Art for Architecture
Ukraine

Art for Architecture
Ukraine

Soviet Modernist Mosaics from 1960 to 1990

Yevgen Nikiforov (Photographs)
Polina Baitsym (Text)

DOM
publishers

Ernest Kotkov (1972), Comprehensive School no. 90, Kyiv

Contents

ВЕСЕЛИЙ

Veselyi Bus Stop (1985), P. Orel. Veselyi, Chernihov Region

A Brief History of Monumental and Decorative Arts in Soviet Ukraine

Polina Baitsym

'For a long time I have cherished the idea which I now lay before you.' According to the account of Anatoly Lunacharsky, with these words Lenin presented to him the Plan for Monumental Propaganda. Lenin was deeply inspired by Tommaso Campanella's *City of the Sun,* where frescoes not only served as visual materials for science and history lessons but also 'aroused civil feelings' and 'participated in the business of raising and educating the new generation.' However, in the context of the Soviet Union, Lenin considered frescoes out of place; statues became the conduits of an educational mission.[1]

Lenin's Plan for Monumental Propaganda, issued in 1918, became the first document that closely linked the artistic environment of the newly created state with its policies. It consisted of two parts: the removal of the tsarist monuments and the elaboration of the projects for monuments which would glorify the October Revolution. The list of figures that was chosen as a basis for sculptors' creations was not limited in ideological terms: it included persons who were not associated with socialism but were defined as 'genuine heroes of culture.' The artists were granted complete freedom in the execution of their monumental objects (they could even choose the place for its installation). The first artworks created within the Plan differed in terms of style: some sculptors were inspired by primitive art, others by Cubism and Futurism.

Lenin's Plan for Monumental Propaganda was a utopian project, the implementation of which was not possible in his lifetime, primarily due to the lack of competent sculptors in the country.[2] However, in the context of monumental and decorative arts, the acceptance of the decree which embodied the Plan in 1918 played an essential role. It predated the expansion of Agitational art in the Soviet Union. The combination of figures, decorative plaques and festive openings of the monuments, complemented by musical performances, showed that the Plan was the first embodiment of the idea of 'synthesis of the arts' in the public spaces. This idea would resurface during the Thaw with an intense emphasis in architecture and monumental and decorative arts.

In 1924 in Ukraine, the artist Mykhaylo Boychuk, just returned from Paris where he resided after his education in Munich and Vienna, became a professor at the Kyiv Art Institute. As the head of the Monumental Art Studios, he took part in the implementation of the Plan. During his professorship, Boychuk established his school, combining Byzantine influence with Ukrainian folk art in monumental and decorative objects. It became well-known as 'Boychukisty.'[3]

Always with Lenin (1968), Vartan Arakelov and Volodymyr Lysychansk, Sosiura House of Culture

In 1930, during the Sixteenth Communist Party Congress, Stalin famously stated that the culture of the Soviet Union should be 'socialist in content and national in form, and would continue to exist as such until the global victory of the proletariat, at which time both of its aspects would become socialist.'[4] He had several ideas in mind for how this 'socialist in content' culture could be achieved. First, the release of the decree of the Central Committee of the Communist Party, 'On the Restructuring of Literary and Artistic Organisations', issued on 23 April 1932, laid the foundation for the institutional framework of cultural production for the country. Following the decree, new organisations should have been established to unite all the creative individuals willing to take part in building the socialist culture. They were to be named creative unions. In the first decades after the decree only three such organisations were founded: The Writers' Union, The Composers' Union, and the Architects' Union. Notwithstanding the fact that the decree 'On the formation the Union of Artists of the USSR' was released in 1939, the Artists' Union was established only in 1957 when the First Congress was convened. The underlying principle of the unions' membership was aesthetic and ideological conformity to Socialist Realism, 'the official method of Soviet art' that was introduced at the First Congress of Soviet Writers in 1934.

As many of the researchers of Soviet art point out, it is easier to define what Socialist Realism was not, than what it actually was.[5] The early definition of Socialist Realism, initially coined in the Charter of the Writers' Union and reproduced in *Pravda*, was as follows:

definition. In 1937 many Boychukists, including Boychuk, were executed. Nevertheless, in the rhetorics of Soviet officials, his case embodied the victory of Soviet art over 'harmful influences of the West', and his name with the negatively connotative label 'Ukrainian bourgeois nationalism' was the spectre that haunted the Ukrainian art world until Perestroika.

Upon this historical background, the Ukrainian Union of Artists was established in 1938. In the institutional charter, validated in 1939, the Union was defined as 'a voluntary organisation that unites on the area of the Ukrainian Soviet Socialist Republic (UkrSSR) workers of visual arts (painters, graphic artists, sculptors, theatre artists and folk-art masters) and individuals who conduct research and critical work in the field of visual art. The First Congress, which was called 'the supreme governing body' in the Charter, was convened with the establishment of the institution in 1938.[8]

The Second World War interrupted the development of the organisational structure that would have put the whole sphere of art production in Ukraine under governmental control. The Second Congress of the Ukrainian Union of Artists took place between 3 and 7 April 1956, right before the First All-Union Congress in 1957. The latter not only marked the establishment of the Union of Artists of the USSR, but also condemned the dogmatism in aspects of art regulation and production of Stalin's era, reasserting the legacy of Socialist Realism. 'The official method of Soviet art' was also revised within the reassessment of Stalinist cultural heritage, already underway in 1955.

Ukrainian art historians consider the Thaw as the period of the rise of monumental and decorative arts, both in terms of quality and quantity. As production of mosaics, reliefs and stained-glass windows was closely linked with the state architectural policies, the resolution of 1955 'On Elimination of Excesses in Design and Construction', initiated by Khrushchev, laid the foundation for the

Socialist Realism, the basic method of Soviet artistic literature and literary criticism, demands truthfulness ('pravdivost') from the artist and a historically concrete portrayal of reality in its revolutionary development. Under these conditions, truthfulness and historical concreteness of artistic portrayal ought to be combined with the task of the ideological remaking and education of labouring people in the spirit of socialism.[6]

Formalism, the umbrella term for abstract art, Cubism, Futurism, Conceptual and Pop Art, Impressionism and other genres that significantly differed from Realism, was fiercely condemned. Religious art, erotic art and political art that did not support the Party line were also banned.[7] The newly established Committee of Artistic Affairs began purging Formalist artists between 1936 and 1938, and the Boychukisty oeuvre fell under the rapid development of the sphere of monumental and decorative arts. The Soviet architects concentrated on the elaboration of typical architectural projects where all bombastic features, associated with Stalinist architecture, were 'eliminated'. Mosaics, stained glass windows and reliefs became the essential means of decoration of standardised buildings which granted the objects 'individuality' and 'architectural expressiveness'.

With the liberalisation of the Soviet art scene, many Ukrainian artists who worked with other mediums (for instance, oil painting, graphics and political postering) turned to monumental and decorative arts, bringing together their vision, experience and skills for the creation of the unique artworks presented in this book.

The Union only partially supervised the production of these mosaics, reliefs and stained-glass windows. Many of the orders were executed through the regional Artistic and Production Workshops, subordinate to the Art Fund, a complementary organisation established in 1940 for assisting the Union in financial issues. Thus, within the postwar large-scale construction of buildings, artists who were not members of the Union were able to procure and execute orders either independently or in 'creative associations'. After the Typical Construction in Ukraine was introduced, the number of objects for decorating significantly increased: the monumentalists created works in interiors and on facades of cultural palaces, factories, cinemas, canteens, shops, kindergartens, schools, etc. Their customers were predominantly industrial enterprises who held as clients schools and public buildings.

From the 1960s to the 1980s, particular attention in the official Soviet discourse was paid to the beauty of the living environment of a Soviet citizen; its 'aestheticisation'. Art in public space was to become a means for raising a 'harmoniously developed' Soviet man and improving his awareness of his environment in its artistic integrity. The rapid ascent of monumental and decorative arts in Ukraine coincided with the launch of Soviet space and nuclear power programs, primarily accompanied by an enthusiastic depiction of satellites, spaceships, cosmonauts, atoms, etc. The new definition of Socialist Realism, imposed in the Union during the Thaw, required Soviet artists to 'address contemporary subjects', avoiding the pomposity of Stalin's era. Idealised images of 'common people' and 'workers' of distinct professions, combined with the romantic picturing of 'harmonious work', flooded Soviet visual culture. Such depictions were widely spread on the facades of industrial enterprises or on the houses and palaces of culture, supervised by the commissioning enterprise. The Pioneer Movement, to which Khrushchev paid particular attention, also became a frequent reference for images placed in children's spaces.[9]

These focuses largely continued in the 1970s and early 1980s when the monumental and decorative arts in Ukraine experienced a downturn. A plethora of low-quality and ideologically loaded artworks were executed at the time. The high numbers of orders, rigid deadlines, scarcity of materials and stressful process to gain approval for sketches hardly contributed to a friendly creative environment. Perestroika marked the shift in stylistic requirements, caused by a slow reconsideration of avant-garde movements' legacies and the rehabilitation of Boychukisty. However, technical issues of production were not solved.

During the period covered in the book, the Ukrainian creative community experienced many changes in state policies for the arts. A notorious case that marked the tightening of censorship in 1964 was the destruction of the stained-glass window, *Shevchenko. Mother*, created by Alla Horska, Luidmyla Semykina, Galyna Zubchenko, Opanas Zalyvaha and Halyna Sevruk for the 150th anniversary of Taras Shevchenko's birth. Another case demonstrating the Soviet Ukraine's censorship mechanism was the destruction of Volodymyr Melnychenko and Ada

Be a Worthy Coeval of Your Era (1978), S. Hladkov,
Vinnytsia, mosaic plaque on European Square

Rybachyk's *The Wall of Memory* in 1982. We do not discuss these cases in the book, but these instances of sharp clashes between artists' need to express their views and the state oppression of creative individuality are important to note.

Nowadays, mosaics from Soviet Ukraine are at risk of destruction. In legal terms they are not defined as artworks; they became the subjects of the law 'On the Condemnation of the Communist and National Socialist (Nazi) Regimes, and Prohibition of Propaganda of Their Symbols,' adopted in 2015 by the Verkhovna Rada (the Ukrainian parliament). The law, initiated by the Ukrainian Institute of National Remembrance, sought to create the legal framework for prohibition of propaganda of regime symbols and establishing the procedure for removal of their symbols. It attempted to 'purify' Ukrainian urban spaces of Soviet symbols, names of Soviet heroes and Soviet festivals. With a set of other laws concentrated on the redefinition of the national narrative so as to present the Soviet Union as the main enemy of Ukraine, the Ukrainian Institute of National Remembrance launched the decommunisation process. It resonated with the symbolic rejection of Soviet legacy, particularly embodied in the collective demolition of monuments to Lenin, begun already during the Maidan. Mosaics that became iconic decoration of the buildings in Ukraine in many cases lost their artistic value to local citizens or private owners who preferred to satisfy their needs (such as heat insulation) at the expense of the artworks' preservation.

For a long time we have cherished the idea of a guide book on Ukrainian mosaics which we now lay before you. It presents the findings of a long-lasting investigation, one that began in 2013. For the descriptions of the mosaics, we combined secondary sources with local press materials, the artists' recollections and archival documents. The latter is currently lacking; information on artworks are often limited to the name of the artists and executors, accompanied with the year of completion. Therefore, the book seizes all available knowledge, incorporating notes into where gaps in our data are present.

We hope this book undermines the simplified perspective on Soviet artistic heritage in Ukraine, where monumental and decorative arts existed at the frontier of Party propaganda and the artistic thirst for experimentation. Therefore, we, the descendants, are left with testimonies of manoeuvring between the state regulation and the artistic inner calling, which, we believe, should be remembered.

Introduction

Yevgen Nikiforov

During the last six years I have been engaged in the search for and documentation of Soviet mosaics in Ukraine. My research has had me visit several hundred settlements across the country. The more I travelled and discovered the land, the less I understood about it. People often ask what Soviet mosaics mean to me: they provide a way to acquaint myself with the culture of the country and the visual code of different cities. Through this code of Soviet Modernist monumental art and architecture I discovered unfamiliar terrain. During Ukraine's Soviet period, many cities and towns were either built from scratch or entirely overhauled; Soviet buildings and mosaics dominated visually. My project documents how the Soviet visual dominance has changed throughout the period of independence, influenced by new social, economic, political, cultural and natural forces.

I took the first photos of the mosaics at the end of 2013 in Kyiv. The pieces were easy to find because the monumental and decorative arts of the capital are well-described. In contrast, I enjoyed the adventure of searching for mosaics in uncharted regions, with neither Google images nor relevant pictures of the terrain on the Internet to help guide my trip. There, mobile phones have no coverage, and other vehicles rarely pass by on the roads. In these places, you feel like an explorer.

The more sites I visited, the more my interest in sharing the artworks grew. The mosaic can tell the attentive viewer myriad significant and unexpected things about the surrounding place. One may scrutinise each panel for a long time, detect the decoded plots and admire how different materials – smalt, ceramics, stone and glass – effectively complement each other. These mosaics are an interwoven part of our culture. And the task of this book is to prove their value both for Ukrainians and for the international audience.

In Ukraine there is no database solely for monumental and decorative arts. I utilised a variety of methods to identify artworks in my exploration. I studied materials in archives and libraries, spoke with monumental artists and searched for images using hashtags on social media. Today my database holds records of more than 5,000 objects, all located in distinct regions of the country. Most of them I was lucky to see with my own eyes and camera. My archive of the monumental and decorative arts created by Soviet Ukrainian artists between the early 1960s and the

Industrial Dnipro (1959-1961), Ivan Lytovchenko, Valerii Lamakh, Ernest Kotkov, River Port, Kyiv

Dnipro Waves (1985), Artist: Ernest Kotkov, Architects: Iurii Khudiakov, Viktor Sudorhin
Dnipro, Meteor Ice Sports Palace

early 1990s is the largest and is quite expansive. This guide allows you to begin your journey through the most impressive artworks I have found during the last six years.

Selecting pieces for the guide took several months. The problem I faced: how do I choose 100 mosaics out of 3,000? The book includes the most sublime artworks and presents the most important artists from each region of Ukraine. There are no kitsch, typical or straightforward mosaics in this book. I focused on technically challenging pieces where artists had space to experiment with designs and materials.

I did not include mosaics which were not open to the public: airports, museum funds, factories and private enterprises. The artworks presented in the guidebook can be seen by anyone. They are always in the public space and guarded by loyal security officers. Unfortunately, no laws protect the monumental and decorative arts of Ukraine. Because of this, there may be locations where the objects are partially or fully destroyed.

Some pieces have been ruined over time and require restoration. Artworks are frequently damaged in the process of local construction projects – the residents do not realise a piece's historical and cultural value. I saw beautiful bus stops with painted-over decorative mosaics. In Ukraine, the bus stops are often used as bulletin boards with self-made advertisements for weatherproofing or wedding photographers. As old Soviet bus stops go out of service, new structures are made of simple and lightweight materials that usually do not protect mosaics and monuments from the rain and wind.

Many good artworks are not included in the guide because their current state is a pitiful semblance of how they originally looked. While preparing the book, I had to exclude two crucial mosaics, one in the Kharkiv region and one in Dnipro. One masterpiece, the volume and spatial sculpture, *Dnipro Waves*, made of smalt and metal, was destroyed by heavy machinery in March 2019. I monthly receive similar news of the destruction of other important works. I am genuinely sorry if you are unable to see some of the pieces shown here during your journey.

The length of each suggested route varies from 1,500 to 2,400 km. They recommend visiting not only the masterpieces of monumental and decorative arts of the 20th century, but also the most interesting geographical points of Ukraine. I sincerely hope that innumerable explorers will dare to discover this country through these routes I have developed.

North

Central Bus Station

1 Demiivska Square, Kyiv

001 A

Ada Rybachuk,
Volodymyr Melnychenko
Blue Bus, Buses, Khreshchatyk
Ceramic mosaic
1961

The mosaics at the Central Bus Station are united by the idea of movement that Ada Rybachuk and Volodymyr Melnychenko intended to convey. The task of decorating the station's interior was reassigned to Rybachuk and Melnychenko when the structure was already in the final stage of construction. Thus, the duo worked with neither approved sketches nor compensation. According to the recollection of Volodymyr Melnychenko, their initial plan was to segregate the inner space visually. They applied a black colour as a background to create the distinct vivid stripes, hoping they would resemble the movement of light at night and the outlines of streets. The artists also featured colourful contours – the silhouettes of buses and cars – which were executed in white, blue and yellow. They chose a turquoise tint for the columns and saturated yellow for the ceiling. Such a combination of colours was 'risky' at the time: it was associated with 'Ukrainian bourgeois nationalism', though, back then, Rybachuk and Melnychenko were not concerned with national issues. They wanted to create 'the atmosphere of festivity'. Initially, the artists hoped to cover the columns in small mosaic chips. However, Stepan Kyrychenko warned them that the slate pillars prevented this. To deal with this, Kyrychenko shared with Rybachuk and Melnychenko his method which involved the application of epoxy mastic. It substantially reduced the amount of work for the artists and resulted in the creation of sutures which the creators liked. The sutures became grounds to accuse Rybachuk and Melnychenko of making Formalist art. The artists created an additional design as a textile at the station which was not approved by the chief architect of the city, Borys Pryimak. Despite not having consent to make these designs for this project, the duo managed to produce them on their own. The daughter of Pryimak liked the result so much that she cut off a piece of the design to use as curtains for her home.

Mosaic Ensemble on Peremohy Avenue

17-27 Peremohy Avenue, Kyiv

002 A

Ivan Lytovchenko, Volodymyr Priadka, Valerii Lamakh, Ernest Kotkov
Trypillian Kyiv (1980), *Kyivan Rus* (1980),
On the Guard of Peace (1968),
Symphony of Labour (1968),
The Ukrainian SSR (1980),
Impulse of Science and Progress (1979)
Smalt mosaic, glass, ceramic mosaic,
natural stone, relief

The oeuvre of the artists who decorated these residential buildings – Ivan Lytovchenko, Volodymyr Priadka, Valerii Lamakh, Ernest Kotkov – considerably shaped the development of monumental and decorative arts in Ukraine. During the Thaw, the artists were able to realise stylistic experiments in the urban environment and architectural decoration after the Typical Construction was introduced.

They applied their experience from distinct creative spheres – the textile industry (Lytovchenko), sculpture (Priadka), and political poster-design (Lamakh and Kotkov) – to the production of mosaic panels and reliefs, so as to achieve a 'synthesis of arts'. In the context of the 'aestheticisation' of roads and the urban environment, the decoration of these residential buildings in Kyiv on Peremohy Avenue was a significant assignment. In 1967 two artist-duos – Lytovchenko and Priadka, and Lamakh and Kotkov – prepared six initial sketches. The execution of two of the artworks, *Symphony of Labour* and *On the Guard of Peace*, were already underway when the artists learned that a department store was in construction nearby and would partially obstruct the view of their mosaic panels. They refused to proceed with the job and left the backgrounds of the panels incomplete. In 10 years, Representatives of the General Directorate for Capital

Construction asked the artists to finish the mosaics; Kyiv was to appear along the Olympic Torch relay's route and they wanted the city to look beautiful and fully finished for the official visitors. They agreed on the condition that the artists would change the style of the panels. Lytovchenko and Priadka were willing to destroy old mosaics and replace them with new ones. Lamakh and Kotkov, however, considered the artworks testimonies to Ukrainian history and insisted on their preservation to publicly illustrate the challenges artists faced in monumental and decorative arts. In the late 1970s, the artists created heraldic compositions depicting the development of Ukraine from the Trypillya period, through the Kyivan Rus, to the end of the Middle Ages (the third and the fourth mosaic panels which should have replaced the artworks of 1967). The last two mosaics, created by Kotkov, portray prospering Socialist Ukraine in an ornamental manner.[1]

A

Shuliavska Subway Station
46 Peremohy Avenue, Kyiv

Ivan Lytovchenko,
Maria Lytovchenko
Generations (1963)
Ceramic mosaic

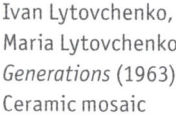

The construction of subway stations was considered an important undertaking for the Soviet officials since the opening of the first prestige project in Moscow in 1935 – the metro system. When Socialist Realism was adopted as 'the method of Soviet architecture' in 1937, the first line of Moscow subways in particular was defined as the architectural project that addressed the needs of the proletariat.[2] Remarkably, propagandistic monumental and decorative artworks were embedded in the design of the second line, opened from 1937-1938.[3] In contrast, the first line stations, as Catherine Cooke points out, 'were purely architectural' (the mosaics of Alexander Deineka and the sculpture of Matvei Manizer were added as parts of the interiors later on). The metro in Kyiv, a project realised with the assistance of the team involved in the construction of Moscow subway stations, was opened on 6 November 1960. It featured 5 platforms: 'Arsenalna', 'Vokzalna', 'Universytet', 'Hreschatyk' and 'Dnipro'. Because the 'Dnipro' platform is above-ground, a special mechanised tunnelling shield was developed by a group of Kyiv geologists and engineers for the proper operation of the transport system. In 1963, the line was supplemented with two stations: 'Politekhnichnyi Instytut' and 'Zavod "Bilshovyk"' (Factory 'Bolshevik', now – 'Shuliavska').[4] The hall of the 'Shuliavska' is covered with brown and beige tiles of two distinct sizes. The transitional lobby of the platform is made with the Typical Construction design (Khrushchev was also closely involved in the building of the Moscow Metro, and this experience may have altered his perspective on Soviet architecture)[5]; it is decorated with grey and blue-green ceramic tiles. The central mosaic depicts two socialist workers on the background of the Red Banner and, presumably, the factory, in heroic poses; one of the figures is holding the atom, symbolically linked to the assertion of the power of the USSR through the nuclear program (in particular during the Thaw, nuclear power plants entered a period of intensive construction).

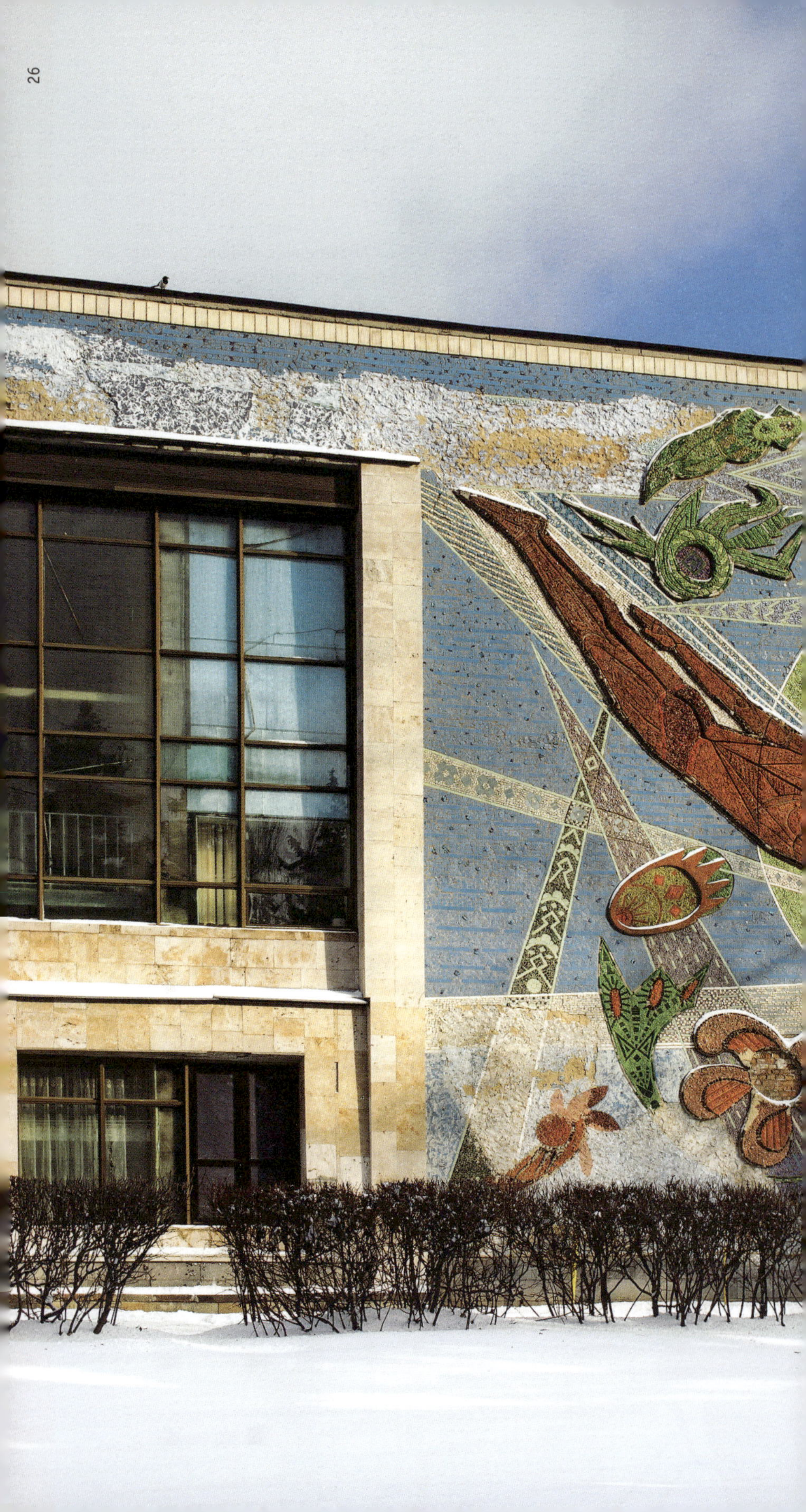

Nauka Sport Complex

32 Akademika Vernadskoho
Boulevard, Kyiv

004 **A**

Halyna Zubchenko,
Hryhorii Pryshedko
Movement (1969)
Smalt mosaic, glass, ceramic mosaic,
natural stone, relief

The mosaic exemplifies the visual combination of science and sports, a relatively rare pairing for Ukrainian monumental and decorative arts. The artists, whose oeuvre is associated with the Sixtiers (*shistdesiatnyky*), elegantly united the subjects in powerful and careening figures of swimmers, framed by lines and circles which structure the composition.

A

Olimpiiska Subway Station
57 Fizkultury Street, Kyiv

005 A

Oleksandr Milovzorov
The Olympics (1982)
Smalt mosaic, relief

The subway station 'Republican Stadium' (now 'Olimpiiska') was opened on 19 December 1981. The opening of the platform was associated with the infamous Olympic Games of 1980 in Moscow, boycotted by the United States and other countries due to the invasion of the Soviet Army into Afghanistan. The Republican Stadium (now The Olympic National Sports Complex), after which the subway station was named, was also reconstructed between 1978 and 1980 specifically for the Olympic Games. The mosaic focuses on the depiction of the Olympic flame that was transferred via a relay system from Greece to Moscow in the period from 19 June to 19 July 1980. The route of the Olympic torch relay included a path through Soviet Ukraine; many objects of monumental and decorative arts were created or updated before the Olympic events occurred (for instance, the boundary markers of the region to guide the torchbearers). Remarkably, the artist did not depict any human figure in the mosaic – rather unusual for Soviet art at the time. In the 1970s and the early 1980s, when polemics between art experts from the USSR and foreign critics erupted,[6] Socialist Realism was presented in the local media as a method that concentrated on humans and admiration for them, while Western modernist art was considered to be oppressive and ignorant of their existence.

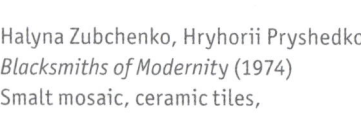

Institute for Nuclear Research of the National Academy of Sciences of Ukraine
47 Nauky Avenue, Kyiv

006 A

Halyna Zubchenko, Hryhorii Pryshedko
Blacksmiths of Modernity (1974)
Smalt mosaic, ceramic tiles,
slag glass ceramic, coloured glass

The Institute for Nuclear Research was established according to a decree from the Council of Ministers of the UkrSSR in 1970. It was founded to research the fields of low and medium energy nuclear physics, the physics of reactors and the use of isotopes and atomic radiation in the agrarian economy.[7] The mosaic on the facade of the Institute was executed by the married couple Halyna Zubchenko and Hryhorii Pryshedko. Despite the ideological conformity of its subject (the rhetorics of admiration for construction of nuclear power plants was embedded in the official Soviet discourse), its style demonstrates a tendency towards abstract and vividly geometric images. The artistic representation of the atom in the centre shapes the composition. Atomic rays are grabbed by red figures, whose forms resonate with the depiction of blacksmiths spread, particularly, in the political posters of the 1920s.[8] On 2 February 1960, the Institute launched the first nuclear reactor in the Ukrainian SSR. According to the recent illuminations of the subject in press, the reactor expired in 2015. This mosaic is one of the most popular among photographers, however, we caution you to be alert when you take photos. Do not forget your ID – it will be incredibly useful if representatives of the Institute security service approach you.

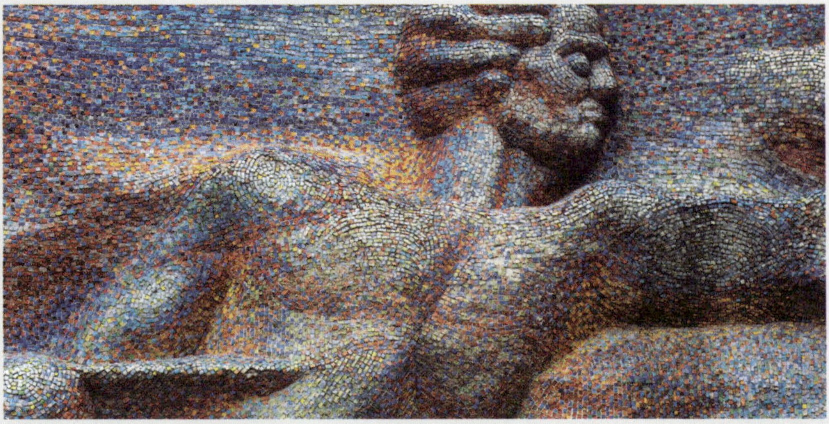

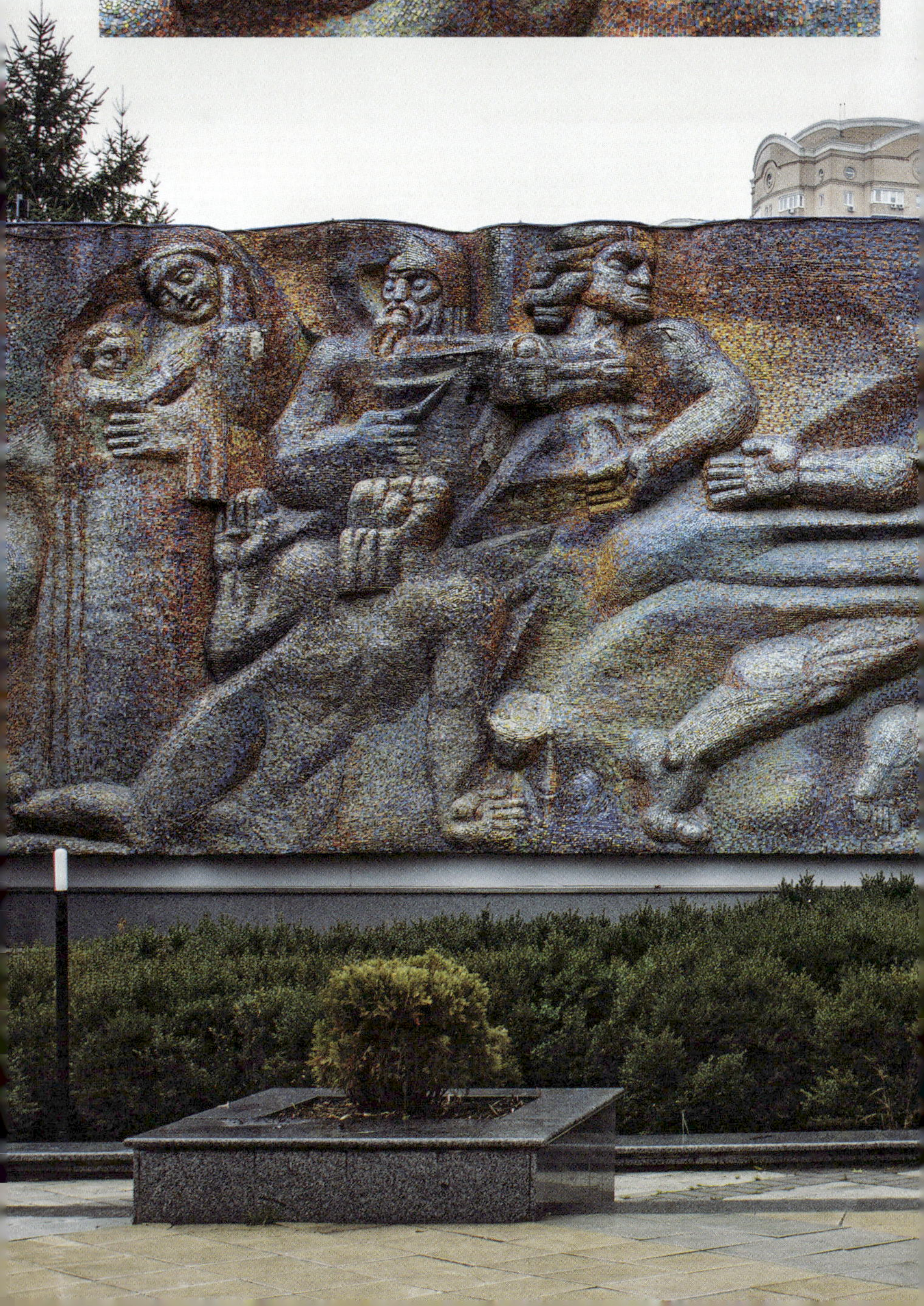

Kyiv Jewellery Factory
17 Holosiivska Street, Kyiv

Iurii Levchenko,
Mykola Kutniakov
Eternal Movement (1980)
Smalt mosaic, relief

007 A

In this relief covered with smalt mosaic, the artists invoked the October Revolution. Though the subject is intrinsic to the doctrine of Socialist Realism, the authors realised it in a visually distinctive style, merging a depiction of human figures with geometric elements and enhanced by an abundance of colours.

A

National Cancer Institute
33 K1 Mykhaila Lomonosova
Street, Kyiv

Halyna Zubchenko,
Hryhorii Pryshedko
Victory (1970–1971)
Smalt mosaic, ceramic tiles,
slag glass ceramic, coloured glass

008 A

This mosaic offers a notable reinterpretation of the idea of victory, a subject that is commonly framed in the context of the Second World War in Soviet art. The artists shiftedd the narrative to the area of health, and depicted a patient who, with their doctors, directs gamma rays onto a black monster, a symbol for disease. Generally, the mosaic references cobalt therapy (the application of gamma radiation from the radioisotope cobalt-60), which was introduced in the Soviet Union in the 1960s.

Kyiv Palace of Children and Youth

13 Lavrska Street, Kyiv

009 A

Ada Rybachuk, Volodymyr Melnychenko
Triptych Wonderful Violin:
Oh Songs of Mine, Oh Songs of Mine,
Dedication to Mariia Prymachenko,
Magical Fiddle (1963-1968),
Children of the World (1963-1968)
Smalt mosaic, relief

The Palace of Children and Youth was built in 1965 following the architectural design of Avraam Miletskyi and Eduard Bilskyi who received the State Award from the USSR for the building. The initial artistic intent was to design the space to embrace all the children's needs. The duo Ada Rybachuk and Volodymyr Melnychenko created the mosaics on the premises (located in different wings of the palace) and the swimming pool. The artworks in the pool were restored in 2019.

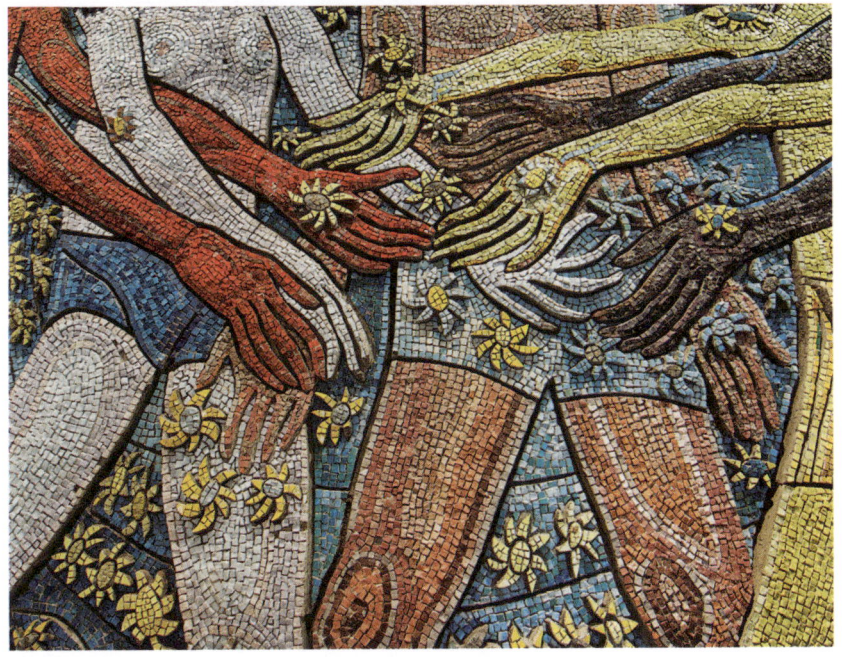

The Bohdan and Varvara Khanenko National Museum of Arts
17 Tereshchenkivska, Kyiv

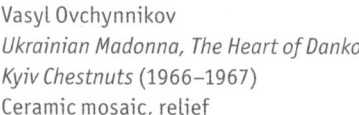

010 A

Vasyl Ovchynnikov
Ukrainian Madonna, The Heart of Danko, Kyiv Chestnuts (1966–1967)
Ceramic mosaic, relief

The Bohdan and Varvara Khanenko Museum of Arts was founded in 1921, when Varvara Khanenko transferred the couple's collection of masterpieces to the newly created Ukrainian Academy of Sciences. It occupies the premises of the Khanenkos' former palace on Tereshchenkivska Street 15–17.[9] The mosaics, located in the yard of the museum, were created by the former head of the institution, Vasyl Ovchynnikov, who occupied the position for 42 years, from 1936 until his death in 1978. In the early 1960s, Ovchynnikov applied for state support for the decoration of the museum exterior. His requests were declined, so the artist decided to create the pieces on his own: Ovchynnikov bought all the materials and executed all the mosaics himself, at his own leisure and discretion. He was the former student of Oleksandr Bohomazov, a representative of the Ukrainian avant-garde movement. Due to his training, Ovchynnikov applied his professor's notion of colour combinations, uniting it with authentic rhythms that highlight the resemblance of the artworks with oil painting.[10] Nowadays, the museum incorporates mosaics into their collection. Some of them can be viewed from the inner yard on Tereshchenkivska Street 15; others are available on Tereshchenkivska Street 17.

The Hall of Glory at the National Museum of the History of Ukraine in the Second World War

Zapecherna Street, Kyiv

011 A

Stepan Kyrychenko,
Roman Kyrychenko, Nadiia Klein
Triumph of Victory (1978–1984)
Smalt mosaic

The Second World War was commemorated in the Soviet Union as 'the Great Patriotic War', where glorification of the victory was emphasised over remembrance of the victims.[11] The Ukrainian State Museum of the History of The Great Patriotic War of 1941–1945 (since 2015, the National Museum of the History of the Second World War) was opened on 17 October 1974; restructured as the Memorial Complex Ukrainian State Museum of the History of the Great Patriotic War of 1941-1945 in 1981 (yes, this is an accurate title). According to the current institutional narrative, the republican exhibition of 1946, *Ukrainian Partisans, Combating German and Fascist Invaders,* laid the foundations for the establishment of the museum.[12] The significance of the victory is clear in the smalt mosaic located in the museum's Hall of Glory. The mosaic was made by this family of artists (Nadiia Klein and Stepan Kyrychenko, along with their son, Roman) who promoted the use of gold- and silver-coloured smalt chips in the decoration of interiors and sculpture. Despite the artwork's dedication to an ideologically loaded subject, the creators concentrated on a schematic depiction of the characters highlighted with colour lines. According to the recollection of the artist Volodymyr Melnychenko, in 1951, when the studio of Anatolii Petrytskyi, the representative of Modernism in Ukrainian art, was destroyed, Stepan along with his assistant Volodymyr Melnyk collected all the stones and mosaic chips which were thrown away and transported them to Kyrychenko's studio. These materials were used in the creation of this mosaic.

A

A

Kyiv Municipal Academic Puppet Theatre
1 Myropilska Street, Kyiv

Hryhorii Dovzhenko
Ancient Kyiv/Kyi, Shchek, Khoryv, and Their Sister Lybid (1970)
Ceramic mosaic, smalt mosaic

012 A

The mosaic depicts the characters who are believed to be the founders of Kyiv – Kyi, Shchek, Khoryv and their sister, Lybid. Created by an artist of great renown, the artwork initially decorated the children's cinema Rovesnyk, the building of which was restructured as the puppet theatre in 1997.

A

Institute of General and Community Hygiene

50 Popudrenka Street, Kyiv

013 A

Volodymyr Bovkun
The 20th Century (1978–1980)
Smalt mosaic, relief

The object on the facade of the Institute of General and Community Hygiene is truly an exceptional case in Ukrainian monumental and decorative arts of the Soviet period. The artist Volodymyr Bovkun combined figurative images with an ornamental background, consisting of parts of the human body. The family with the small boy holding the flower in the centre is framed with enormous hands, referring to the gentle and caring attitude of the subject towards both humans and plants. One may notice that the artwork features small sea inhabitants – this alludes to the activities of the members of the Institute who not only researched and established the sanitary norms for citizens but also studied environmental issues. In the creation of the object, Bovkun invented a distinct reinterpretation of the humanism in Soviet art that allowed him to redefine the notion of 'real', reaching a surrealistic tone in the decoration of the facade.

Children's Library no. 118 and Sports Club
15/1 Malyshka Street,
25/1 Malyshka Street, Kyiv

Mykola Storozhenko
Protecting Nature and Work of the Soviet People (1977–1978)
Smalt mosaic, relief

014 A

The artist Mykola Storozhenko in the 1970s had an ambiguous ideological position, as he depicted Ukrainian scholars and cultural agents in his oeuvre, while also referencing to religious subjects. Though the mosaics convey the idea of harmony between nature and work, common for the Soviet monumental and decorative arts, its visualisation, arranged by geometric contours and curves, is distinct from Socialist Realist guidelines.

Tourist Hotel
2 Raisy Okipnoi Street, Kyiv

Halyna Sevruk
The City on Seven Hills (1986)
Chamotte, ceramic glaze,
enamel, ceramic relief

The panel at the Tourist Hotel unravels the history of Kyiv, portraying recognisable characters of its founders and rulers, local chroniclers and several men of the church. The artist complemented the motley composition with fantastic birds and animals.

Prypiat Complex Design

4, 4A Kurchatova Street 4
6, 12, 22 Lenina Avenue, Prypiat

 016 A

Ivan Lytovchenko
To The Light, Creation, Sunrise,
Music, Energy (1975–1982)
Smalt mosaic, sculptural relief

Ivan Lytovchenko created this mosaic after he was appointed as the head of the decoration of the urban settlement Prypiat. The assignment he received was extremely significant; the city was constructed as the vessel for the biggest nuclear power plant in Europe and the transition point for production transportation. In fact, Lytovchenko took part in the creation of the Soviet utopian project – an idealised industrial city where the citizens live in harmony with their jobs and urban environment, the tiny model of the coveted Soviet Union. The microdistricts of the city were radially constructed around the centre. Lytovchenko decorated the facades of three residential buildings, the cinema and the music school with these objects, incorporating the utopian vision of the city's future and demonstrating his unwillingness to make ideological art. The design features an abundance of highly abstract artworks that tackle the subjects of light and energy, occasionally supplemented with fragments of figurative images. These mosaics are special not only because of their epic scale, but also due to the technological advancement they show: Lytovchenko used metal elements with smalt mosaic chips, and the combination of materials allowed him to achieve changes of the surface colouring in relation to its lighting. For the artist, the tragedy of Chornobyl was deeply personal – he had devoted almost 10 years of his life to the artistic design of the city. Nowadays, the artworks have been destroyed by rain and snow, overgrown with bushes and trees. After Chornobyl's disaster, it was impossible to disassemble and transport the mosaics as the region was dangerous; the primary reason for the artworks' destruction is radiation, absorbed by the smalt and metal.

Yunist Youth Athletic Centre 017 A
110 Peremohy Avenue, Chernihiv

Volodymyr Zinchenko (1975)
Smalt mosaic

In the early years after the October Revolution, the Party put many efforts into 'the creation of the new Soviet man', brought up in the newly established state of the Soviet Union. The role model for such a utopian project originated from the novel, *What is to Be Done?*, written by Russian philosopher Nikolai Chernyshevsky in 1863. The commitment, ascesis and strong physical condition of the character Rakhmetov, a revolutionary, inspired many Bolsheviks including Lenin. Consequently, new citizens of the USSR were meant to have a robust and muscular body that would allow them to take part in intense manual labour. In the 1920s, this idea resonated with the agenda of avant-garde movements.[13] The representation of sports in Soviet visual culture took many forms in different periods, altered by the idea of a sound and sturdy citizen-body. As Mike O'Mahony

points out, from the 1960s to the dissolution of the Soviet Union, the subject of physical culture disappeared from the oeuvre of well-established Soviet artists.[14] Furthermore, its depictions became widely associated with ideological conformism. The exception which O'Mahony indicates is the Olympic Games of 1980.[15] We suggest that the creation of the mosaic on the facade of the Chernihiv Yunist Youth Athletic Centre was linked with the corresponding preparation arrangements of the 1980 Olympics. The creators of the objects portrayed young people (in the representations, youth is another feature of the new citizen's body) who participate in various Olympic sports. The framework for the characters' activities resembles a textile, an unconventional artistic solution in the context of Ukrainian monumental and decorative arts. The visual division of the figures from the vivid pattern of the background is achieved with the thick dark contouring. The mosaic is not flat; the chiaroscuros (an effect of contrasted light and shadow) in the execution of the figures of the young people resemble oil painting techniques.

A

House of Culture
2 Miroshnyka Street, Ploske

Unknown artist
Ceramic mosaic, smalt mosaic

018 A

This artwork refers to the 1917 October Revolution, which was a common subject in Soviet art. The distinct feature of the panel is the turquoise contouring of the horse's mane and tail, which undermines the requirement of realistic depiction inherent to Socialist Realism.

Myrhorod Palace of Culture
019 A

112 Hoholya Street, Myrhorod

Stepan Kyrychenko,
Roman Kyrychenko
The Genius of Mykola Hohol (1973)
Smalt mosaic

Houses of culture, as workers' clubs, established in the years after the October Revolution, were institutional means put in service by the Party for the shaping of leisure of Soviet citizens. Notwithstanding the fact their role, operation and architecture were the subjects of continuous debates, especially in the 1920s and 1930s, such places provided workers and their families opportunities to socialise and read.[16] The hall of the house of culture in Myrhorod is decorated with mosaics that depict the portrait of Mykola Hohol (the writer who was born in the Myrhorod region) and the characters of his literary works. Nowadays, Hohol's heritage and its incorporation either in Ukrainian or Russian cultural narratives is a subject of intensive polemics. Nevertheless, in the Soviet Union the writer was considered a forerunner of Soviet literature.[17] In the mosaics, his portrait resembles a frontispiece, commonly used in book design. Such an artistic method may have been chosen not only due to the fact that the artists were basically creating monumental illustrations to the literary works but also in recognition of the their experience in design and graphics. Both father and son, Stepan and Roman, like many Ukrainian artists of this period, worked with distinct mediums, including political poster, oil painting and ceramics.

A

Complex Design of the Village Centre

Central Square, Skorodystyk

020 A

Y. Kovtun (1973–1974)
Ceramic mosaic, smalt mosaic

The establishment and expansion of the institutional network for professional artists (through regional unions and regional art funds) was widely accompanied by the development of organisations that supported amateur (*samodiialne*) art in the villages. The amateur artists, though they were considered secondary to and were less celebrated than those who received special training, organised their own festivals, took part in exhibitions arranged by the regional union and were frequently involved in the decoration of their newly built settlements. The amateur art of the Soviet Union is a largely understudied subject; particularly in Ukraine, the large body of work requires further investigation. During the creation of this book, we encountered rare testimonies that the oeuvre of amateur artists tended towards Ukrainian folk art and shared naive and primitive features. We may suppose that in the decoration of Skorodystyk, the amateurs of the village took part at least as executors. In terms of financial support, as in many Ukrainian villages, there was likely an enthusiastic head of *kolhosp* (a collective farm, generally known as a *kolhoz*) who aspired to beautify central buildings of the town. The design of Skorodystyk consists of distinct mosaics that stylistically feature Ukrainian folk art. Additionally, in the early 1970s, the image of Lenin flooded Soviet visual culture to commemorate the 100th anniversary of his birthday, which was celebrated on a grand scale all over the country for the entire decade.

![Ceramic mosaic of Lenin with the dates 1870 × 1970]

A

Kosmos Cinema

5 Polyova Square, Zhytomyr

021 A

Artist: Oleksandr Kostiuk,
Architect: Vasyl Mykytenko
Space Constellation (1987)
Smalt mosaic, stainless steel

The facade of the Kosmos Cinema, the project of the architect Vasyl Mykytenko, is decorated with the smalt mosaic *Space Constellation*, which follows Oleksandr Kostiuk's 1987 sketch of the same name. The artist's approach to the subject of space exploration, which rapidly penetrated Soviet art in the 1960s (and was often combined with the institutional embodiment of the 'most important art' – cinemas), is significantly distinct from other representations of the achievements of the space program in the Soviet culture. Space discourse was generally focused on the image of individuals and changed the rhetoric of their heroism from emphasising the linkage between the people in the 1960s to the tangible distance from them at the beginning of the 1980s.[18] In the design of *Space Constellation*, Kostiuk refused to depict a person and focused on the transmission of the infinity of cosmic space, achieved through the application of curved lines, different shades of blue and the play with colour saturation. The artist's decisions resonated with the demythologisation of the Soviet space program that occurred in the Perestroika period as a result of the publication of personal diaries of crew members and engineering teams.[19] Kostiuk successfully used the excess of the space to accentuate the compositions of stainless steel that embody different constellations. The soft yellow glare of their stars amalgamates the green and lilac colours that fill the space, formed by the curves that resemble petals.

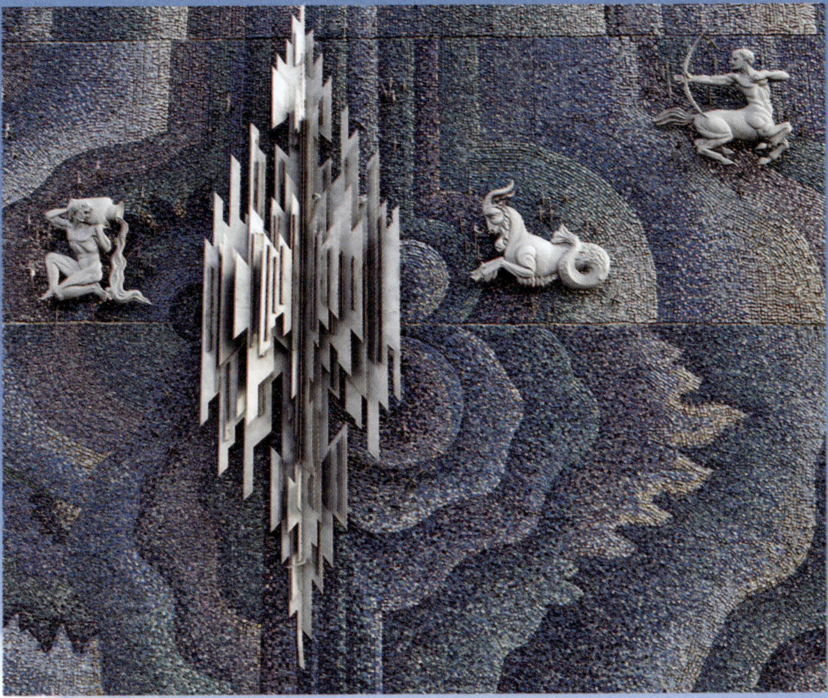

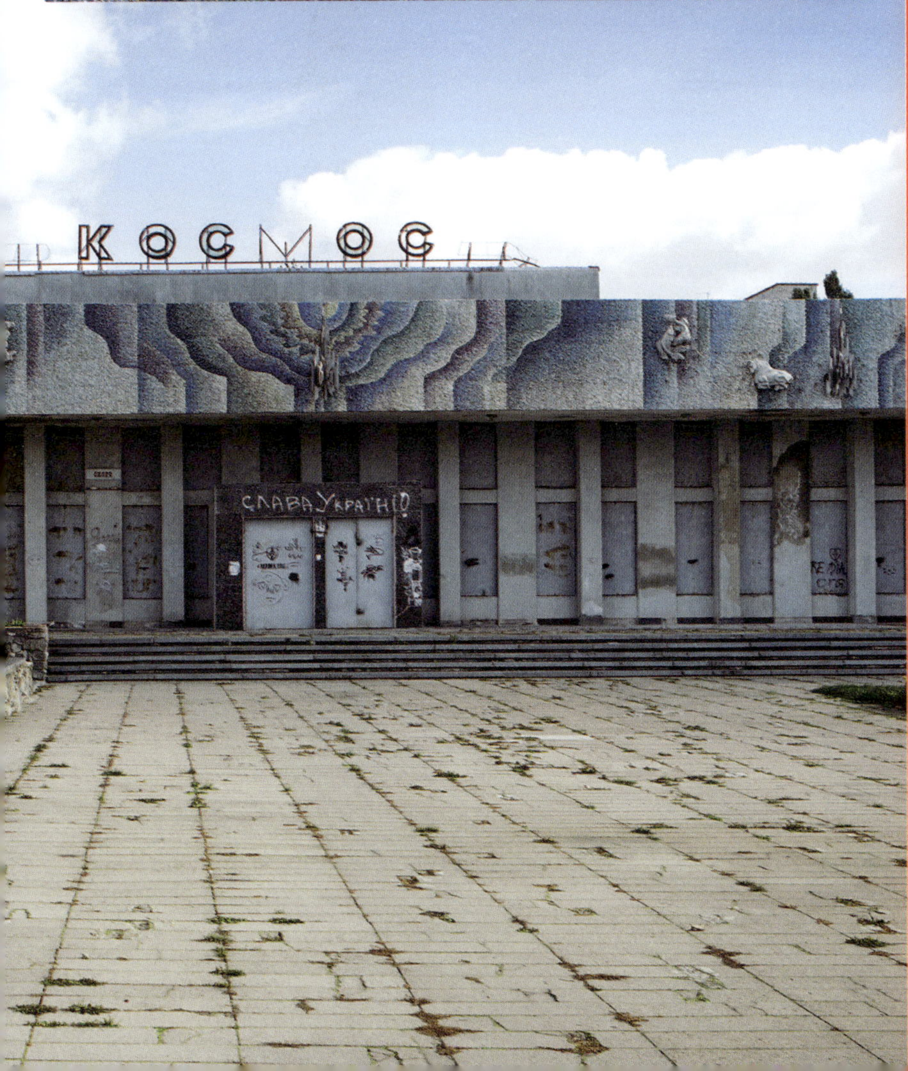
КОСМОС
СЛАВА УКРАЇНІ!

Zhytomyr State Technological University

103 Chudnivska Street, Zhytomyr

Artist: Oleksandr Vorona
Executors: V.Paskov, M. Hitelman, N. Khazanovych
Science (1978)
Ceramic mosaic, smalt mosaic

The Zhytomyr State Technological University was established in accordance with the 84th decree of the Ministry of Higher and Secondary Education of the UkrSSR, 'On Organisation of the Engineering Factories'. The necessity to bring up a new generation of specialists in the post-war period was tightly linked with the restoration of the industrial enterprises, the need to restructure the operation of factories and the aspiration to ease and boost production cycles. Initially in 1960, the faculty was located at the premises of the local pedagogical institute; in 1966 it was granted its own research campus. This building, the main campus, was constructed in the early 1970s: the first laboratories were relocated here in 1972. Its expansion was largely supported by the investments of local industrial enterprises, who recruited the students directly after their graduation. In 1975 the University was reorganised into the regional branch of the Kyiv Polytechnic Institute, which was not only a sign of recognition for the school, but was also a promotion in terms of classification applied to educational facilities.[20] The panel depicts the various professions that one could obtain within the University's program, matching precisely the official discourse of 'scientifically-oriented society'. Remarkably, the characters are portrayed on a background comprised of shapeless spots of striking colours, with complete disregard for Socialist Realist requirements.

Korosten Twine and Rope Factory

12 Heroiv Chornobylia Street, Korosten

023 A

Liubov Smirnova, Zinaida Mosiichuk
Labour (1979)
Ceramic mosaic

The essential feature of the Ukrainian monumental and decorative arts between the 1960s and the 1980s was the large-scale decoration of the facades of buildings – the movement of artworks from the space of interiors to the space of streets. In the creation of such objects at industrial enterprises, artists had to focus on the appearance of their objects from different angles: works were considered good if they took into account the general impression of the viewer both from the landscape perspective and from close-up scrutiny. The premises of the Korosten Twine and Rope factory are currently abandoned. Its facade, as well as a large number of facades of industrial enterprises, was decorated with mosaics to mark the function of the building in the general landscape of the city (especially in Korosten where in the Soviet era there was a developed industry). In terms of subject, the panel is quite typical for the Soviet monumental arts – an idealised image of the workers' daily life. The balanced composition in the ornamental frame, inherent in Mosiichuk's style, is solved in a calm colour scheme. The main emphasis of the mosaic is the flower of flax which symbolises the harmony of the characters with their work. In the Zhytomyr region, flax was especially important: for example, the construction of the Zhytomyr Flax Plant in 1959 contributed to the acceleration of industrialisation in the city and the outlying regions.

A

House of Science and Technology

38/2 Shevchenko Street, Korosten

Unknown artist (1970)
Ceramic mosaic, relief

024 A

The decoration of the facade of the former House of Culture of Railroaders in Korosten is rather unusual: it does not depict the workers of a particular profession. The artists portray characters in national clothes and with Ukrainian folk instruments – a bandura and a sopilka. Another distinctive element of this artwork is the application of relief in order to form the chest of the female figures.

West

Kamianets-Podilskyi

037 Administrative Building

Vinnytsia

038 Vinnytsia National Technological University

Khmilnyk

039 Podillia Sanatorium

Khmelnytskyi

040 Mykhailo Chekman Park for Culture and Recreation

Ternopil

041 Palace of Sports (former Komsomolets Cinema)

042 Teksterno Textile Factory

Shepetivka

043 Mykola Ostrovsky Regional Literary Memorial Museum

Netishyn

044 Horyn Hotel

Rivne

045 Rivne Plant of High-Voltage Gear

Lutsk

046 Lutsk Driving School of the Ukrainian Defense Society

Volodymyr-Volynskyi

047 Bus stop Sugar Factory

Novovolynsk

048 Shakhtar House of Sport

Okean Store

26A Volodymyra Velykoho
Street, Lviv

025 B

Volodymyr Patyk
Sea and Fishes (1982)
Smalt mosaic, relief

The Brezhnev era in the history of the Soviet Union marks the period of the development of personal consumption, embodied in the state policies and supported by Soviet leadership. During this time particularly, the consumption of food and commodities sharply increased.[21] Despite this, fish was still a relatively rare food product, and the construction of the specialised sale location may have eased its distribution. The first fish store in Lviv Ocean was designed by the architects Vasyl Kamenshchyk and Yaroslav Mastylo and opened in 1982. The shop featured a bar – an extraordinary presence in the context of Soviet grocery spaces (and it also may explain its popularity among the local citizens).[22] The mosaic, created by the artist Volodymyr Patyk, is also very uncommon from the perspective of the Soviet monumental and decorative arts. It lacks any ideological message and exploits a style which challenges the essential requirement of Socialist Realism – realistic depiction. We may only assume how the construction of this mosaic, which totally fits the definition of 'Formalism',

was approved. The censorship in arts was tightly focused on places where propaganda was the means of educating and uniting the people – museums, schools, factories, etc. Thus, we may suppose that the decoration of the fish store was relatively insignificant. While we were creating the book, the mosaic was destroyed by the citizens who privatised the shop, despite the promises of chief architect Lviv Yulian Chaplinskyi that the mosaic would be preserved.

B

Ivan Franko National University of Lviv, the Faculty of Cinema and Choreography (former House of Culture)

026 B

16 Stefanyka Street, Lviv

Mykola Krystopchuk (1964)
Ceramic mosaic, smalt mosaic, relief, concrete

The artist portrayed characters who are frequent heroes of panels at houses of culture – workers and children. Such depictions embodied the intention behind the establishment of these institutions: to educate local citizens while providing leisure activities. As the building was formerly used as the builders' house of culture, the artwork depicts their job amidst urban construction. The artist used sgraffito, relief and mosaic to create the piece.

B

Trade Unions' House of Culture 027 B

3 Ruska Street, Uzhhorod

Artist: Attila Dunchak
Executors: Attila Dunchak,
Petro Feldeshi, Volodymyr Bazan
Peaceful Labour (1982)
Smalt mosaic

The trade unions were responsible for the regulation of labour activities and the distribution of social benefits among workers. In different political periods of the Soviet Union, the degree of their independence from the Party and the subtleties of their operation varied. Particularly in the post-war period, trade unions were also in charge of the leisure and cultural involvement of workers. They often supervised the agendas of houses of culture.[23] The mosaic in the Trade Unions' House of Culture in Uzhhorod is a notable example of monumental artwork which challenges Socialist Realist requirements. The only thing that may be considered an element of ideological conformity is the title, *Peaceful Labour,* rooted in the doctrine of 'peaceful coexistence', widely spread since Khrushchev's times. The creator of the mosaic, Attila Dunchak, upon graduation from Uzhhorod College of Applied Arts in 1959 (currently – the Transcarpathian Art Institute), moved to Leningrad in order to pursue his education where the Thaw in the art sphere was already underway. There the artist studied at the prestigious Vera Muhina Higher Artistic and Industrial School (currently – the Saint Petersburg Stieglitz State Academy of Art and Design; one of the oldest educational facilities in Russia), exploring glass and ceramics technologies.[24] After his second graduation, Dunchak returned to Uzhhorod and became a professor at his alma mater. During his tenure, he created new courses that promoted the use of ceramics for volumetric and spatial plastic arts in urban environments.[25] As in a plethora of Dunchak's artworks, here the artist combined extremely schematic depictions of characters (the workers who participate in different cultural activities) with a vivid colour palette. He emigrated to Slovakia in the same year when the object was executed. Nowadays, the Trade Unions' House of Culture is a subject of intense polemics between the representatives of the regional court, who insist on the transfer of the building to their supervision in order to fill the gap in work-sites, and the representatives of regional trade unions, who have owned the house for more than 55 years.

**Administration Building
of Uzhhorod
National University**

3 Narodna Square, Uzhhorod

Ivan Ilko
To Knowledge (1975)
Smalt mosaic, ceramic mosaic

028 B

Ivan Ilko is an artist of Transcarpathian origin who, throughout his oeuvre, applied the approach of an oil painter to the creation of monumental arts. This artwork, which symbolises the enthusiastic aspiration of all people of the Soviet Union to acquire new knowledge, is a peculiar example of his artistic practice. In the 1990s, during the first wave of decommunisation, the section of the panel with the portraits of Lenin and Marx was concealed with a banner bearing the inscription 'The Decree of the President of Ukraine'.

Geologists' Palace of Culture 029 B

17 Geologiv Avenue, Berehove

Mykhailo Mytryk,
Mykhailo Popovych
Geologists (1982)
Smalt mosaic

In the 1970s, the Party's attention to the activities of the palaces and the houses of culture increased significantly. Anne White mentions that the Soviet books on culture and leisure that were published between 1971 and 1982 frequently quoted the statement of Brezhnev, articulated during the 15th Trade Union Congress, that 'free time was not time free from responsibility towards society'.[26] In establishing the palaces of culture, the authorities often referred to professions common in the building's surrounding region. This tendency is exemplified in the palace of culture in Berehove (the name, preferred by the local citizens, is Berehovo), located in the district with the title 'Geologist'. The construction activities in the area started in the 1960s, coinciding with the operation of the

Transcarpathian Geological Expedition that took place exactly in Berehovo. Such a visual representation of the profession showed respect to manual workers. Many of the mosaics, dedicated to the proletariat, depicted men exclusively regardless of the actual involvement of women in the profession. However, this mosaic does show a woman whose appearance may be linked to the head of the Transcarpathian Geological Expedition in Berehovo for over 10 years, the geologist, Vira Zaitseva. Nowadays, the building is up for sale with a price of 180,000 euros.

B

House of Culture

1 Fabrychna Street, Volovets

Unknown artist (1975)
Ceramic mosaic, slag glass

The facade of the house of culture in Volovets is decorated with a mosaic which, despite the fact it pictures workers, was created in a peculiar schematic style. It refers to Transcarpathian visual culture, employing regional folk ornaments. Similar to the panel on the facade, the interior mosaic demonstrates the achievements of the Soviet Union.

Palace of Culture of the Power Engineers

47 Mitskevycha Street, Burshtyn

031 B

Yurii Alieksandrov,
Viktor Elkonin
Prometheus (1974)
Smalt mosaic, relief

As it was already mentioned, the palaces and houses of culture were means of organising the leisure of workers in the most 'efficient and appropriate' way. Nevertheless, during the Thaw these places occasionally served as locations for unofficial exhibitions or even jazz dances, due to the complex bureaucratic system of their supervision. The relief, covered with smalt mosaic, exemplifies the tendencies of Soviet art commonly associated with the Thaw, though it was executed in 1974. The schematic depiction of Prometheus embodies the idea of bringing the light to people by power engineers; the geometric shapes of the relief and the colouring of the mosaic represent those stylistic elements which were considered to be abandoned within the doctrine of Socialist Realism. The fact that one of the creators, Viktor Elkonin, was a well-established Soviet artist within the so-called 'official' art scene hints at the methods Soviet monumentalists used to combat censorship in their oeuvre.

B

Ivan Franko Regional Academic Ukrainian Musical Drama Theatre in Ivano-Frankivsk

032 B

42 Nezalezhnosti Street,
Ivano-Frankivsk

Vasyl Vilshuk, Yosyp Kosovych,
Mykhailo Murafa, Oleksandr Medviedev
(1979–1981)
Ceramics

The Ivan Franko Musical Drama Theatre in Ivano-Frankivsk was established in 1939 to unite several wandering troupes; initially, it was located in the premises of regional philharmonic. The hall of the current building of the theatre (which was opened in 1982) is decorated with a gigantic ceramic panel.[27] The artwork unites various episodes of daily life, historical plots and folklore of the region within the aesthetic style derived from Hutsul visual culture. According to the recollection of Mykhailo Murafa, the supervisor of the group Vasyl Vilshuk invented the idea for the decoration at first, and each of the artists developed it on their own. The work on the object was conducted in Lviv at the factory of industrial ceramics. However, the separate pieces of the panel were put together on-site. It is worth mentioning that three of the artists – Vasyl Vilshuk, Yosyp Kosovych and Mykhailo Murafa – portrayed themselves as Hutsuls with sopilkas (a Ukrainian folk woodwind instrument) on one of the ceramic tiles of the panel. Modest colour usage (the artists dyed some fragments of the beige tiles in green) allowed them to balance the abundance of the details with the scale of the ceramic panel.[28]

B

Art Production Kombinat (Workshops)

51/2 Nezalezhnosti Street,
Ivano-Frankivsk

033 B

Valentyn Danyliuk (1967)
Smalt mosaic, relief, concrete

Art production workshops were organisations supervised by the Ukraine Art Fund, which was established in 1940 in order to provide financial and administrative support to the Unions of Artists in the republics. The workshops were responsible for the distribution of orders on monumental and decorative arts in the region. Each workshop provided an opportunity for local artists – including individuals who were not members of the Unions – to earn money for the execution of mosaics, reliefs, stained glass windows, ceramics, etc. Valentin Danyiluk decorated the building of the Art Production Kombinat in Ivano-Frankivsk; he worked there at the time. Supposedly, these workshops concentrated on the production and distribution of tableware, thus the artist pictured workers with their artworks and tools respectively. He managed to avoid using any propagandistic symbols in the mosaic. In 2012, Danyiluk, after the decrease of his veteran pension, was sued because he attempted to add Stalin's moustache to the banner with the face of Viktor Yanukovych, the President of Ukraine at the time. This action was covered as heroic in the local media.[29]

Post Office

6 Ivana Franka Street,
Verkhovyna

Unknown artist
Ceramic mosaic, smalt mosaic,
broken ceramic ware

The mosaic portrays local citizens and
the elements of their daily life, through
Hutsul visual language (Verkhovyna is
considered the centre of Hutsul culture).
The distinct feature of the piece lies in the
fact that the artists used broken ceramic
ware as a robust material.

Village Council (former Kolhosp Office)

156 Shevchenko Street, Mamaivtsi

Unknown artist
Smalt mosaic

035 B

The panel depicts a woman in Ukrainian national costume and a chaplet, personifying Ukraine, under the banner of the Soviet Union. The colouring of the mosaic and the artists' work with lighting resemble oil painting technique.

B

Kolos Stadium
59A Vasylieva Street, Khotyn

Unknown artist
Sport (1987)
Ceramic mosaic

036 B

The decoration of the facade of Kolos Stadium violates the requirements of the Socialist Realism doctrine. The schematic depiction of the characters, involved in sports activities, and the composition, structured with the numberless mono-tone figures, resemble the artworks of avant-garde artists of the early 1920s.

14:5
98
10.2

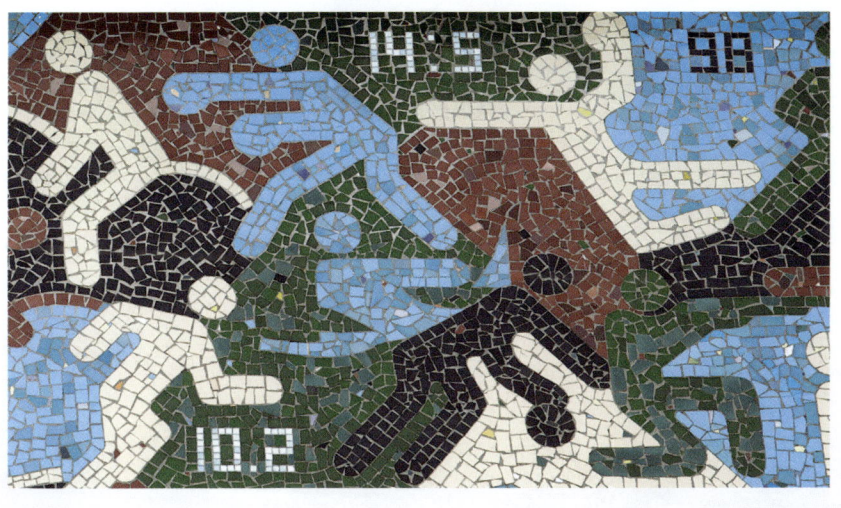

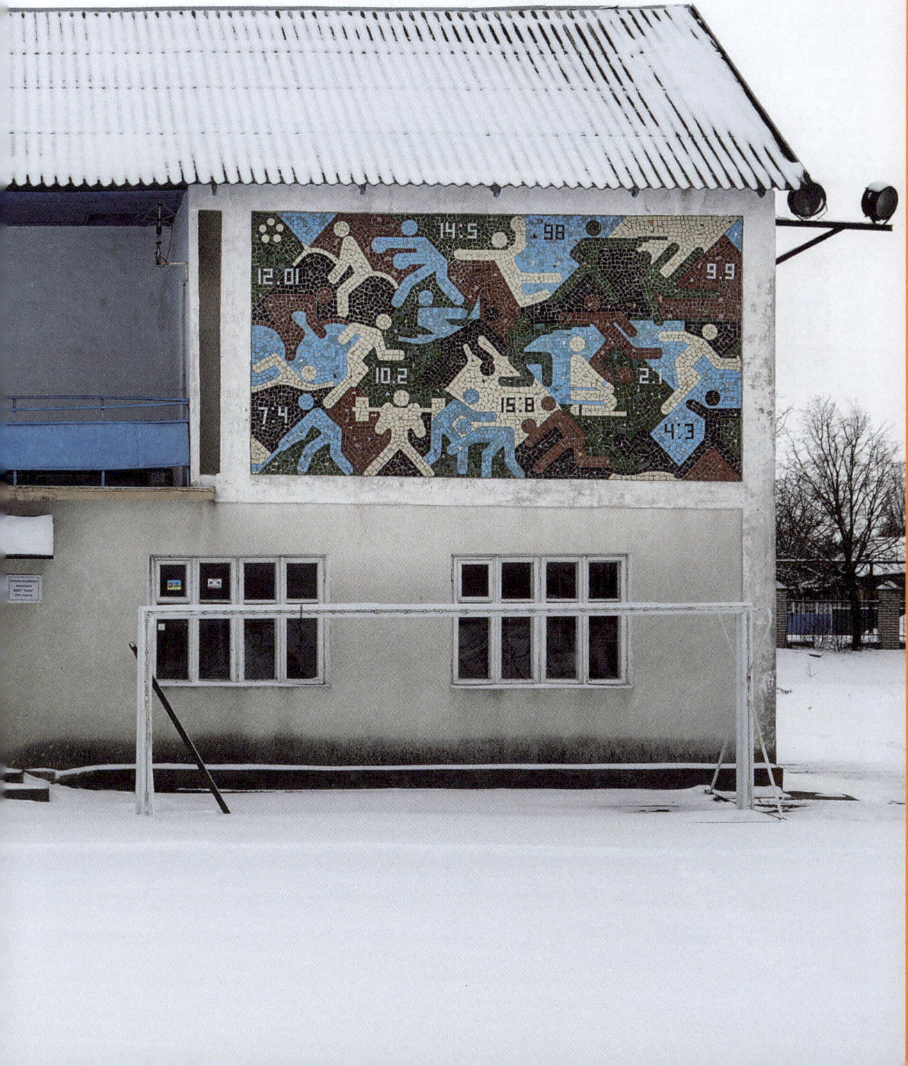
14:5
98
12.01
9.9
10.2
2.1
7.4
15.8
4:3

Administrative Building

037 B

13 Knyazya Volodymyra Street,
Kamianets-Podilskyi

Unknown artist
Ceramic mosaic, granite,
natural stone

This mosaic is a notable illustration of the application of natural stone in Ukrainian monumental and decorative arts. The lines, used by the artist as a primary means of expressiveness, is an elegant solution that requires the creator to have a deep comprehension of compositional balance. In the context of Ukrainian mosaics, it is rather an extraordinary approach.

Vinnytsia National Technological University

93 Khmelnytske Highway, Vinnytsia

Volodymyr Yamkovenko
Science (1986)
Smalt mosaic

038 B

This panel portrays Soviet scholars, the depiction of which is consistent with the representation of the Soviet Union as a progressive and scientific society, as the basic constituents of official discourse. The background of the artwork is composed of the geometric blocks of different colours that resonate with abstract tendencies in art.

B

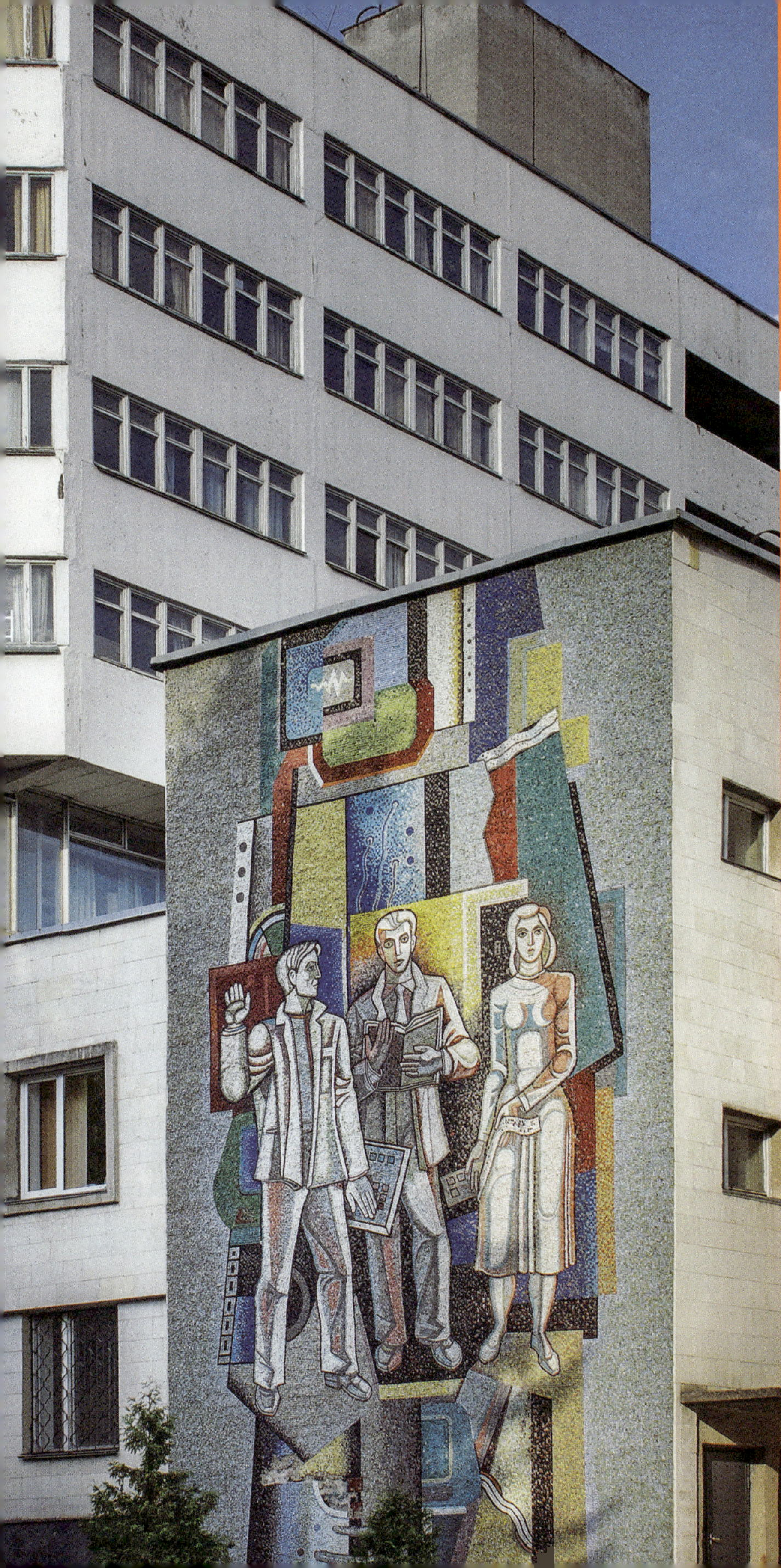

Podillia Sanatorium
10 Kurortna Street, Khmilnyk

Unknown artist (1973)
Ceramic mosaic, smalt mosaic

039 B

The mosaic on the facade of the sanatorium is dedicated to the agrarian achievements of Soviet Ukraine. The woman, depicted in traditional dress, carries bread and a towel, which are the symbols of hospitality that originate in Ukrainian folk traditions.

Mykhailo Chekman Park for Culture and Recreation
1 Parkova Street, Khmelnytskyi

040 B

Mykola Mazur
Filling Station (1981), *Crossover* (1982)
Smalt mosaic, concrete, iron, welding

The oeuvre of Mykola Mazur consists of a unique combination of sculptural and mosaic art, all embedded within the urban environment. His objects feature modernist architectural forms, and resemble imaginative inventions that lack defined functions.

Palace of Sports (former Komsomolets Cinema)

041 B

2 Danyla Halytskoho Boulevard, Ternopil

Dmytro Sheinoha
Golden September (1970s)
Smalt mosaic, relief

This mosaic refers to the events of September 1939, which remain a controversial subject in the national historical narrative. 'Golden September' is a term which was used in Soviet propaganda in order to promote the view that the Red Army's occupation of western areas of Ukraine and Belarus was 'a liberation campaign' against the Polish government's suppression of national minorities. Particularly, this event marked the Soviet intervention into the Second World War. This mosaic was one of the first artworks executed by the artist of the local origin in Ternopil. Legend says that Dmytro Sheinoha installed the object on his own because he did not trust contractors. The thoroughness of the artist's work is believed to have preserved the panel for a very long time. One of the biggest mosaics in the city, the artwork, though representing the Soviet historical narrative, has the potential for symbolic redefinition, taking into account its style, which vividly challenges the Party's views on art.[30]

B

Teksterno Textile Factory
16 Tekstylna Street, Ternopil

042 B

Valerii Lamakh
Six-figure Composition with the Ornamental Frieze, Ornamental Frieze with Elements of the Scheme of the Universe, Friendship (1974–1975)
Smalt mosaic

The textile factory in Ternopil was the last industrial enterprise that Valerii Lamakh decorated before he died. In contrast to his previous experience, these objects the artist created on his own. The execution of the mosaics coincided with an intensive period of work on *The Book of Schemes,* which Lamakh started in 1969.[31] The manuscript, which was arranged and issued posthumously in 2015, united the artist's views on art and featured his theoretical elaborations on the schemes of the universe. The latter Lamakh considered as 'the circles of eternal returning', where 'eternity' was perceived not as 'infinity', but rather as 'a stable feature where even the moment possesses eternity.'[32] In the manuscript, Lamakh discusses many epochs (antiquity, Renaissance, etc.) styles (Gothic, abstract art, etc.) and artists (Pablo Picasso, Kazimir Malevich, Wassily Kandinsky, Paul Cézanne, Henri Matisse, Piet Mondrian). He attempted to create a theory that would promote a special outlook; he linked his ideas with the subject of God, the Creator, asserting that the schemes trace the way to comprehend him. Some of Lamakh's statements provoke ambiguous interpretations: he considered Socialist Realism as 'spiritual art', which is based on 'schematic art'.[33] In the decoration of the textile factory, the artist features schemes that took the shape of ornamental rhombi in the spaces between the representations of all the professions involved in textile production. Lamakh's characters may be easily distinguished from prevalent depictions of workers by the artistic style chosen to portray them. The figures resemble religious images, and this similitude adds a new connotation to its subject, the celebration of labour, embedded in Soviet visual culture. Additionally, Lamakh visually joined the rhombi in the frieze with the characters by maintaining a consistent colour palette.

Mykola Ostrovsky Regional Literary Memorial Museum

2 Ostrovskoho Street, Shepetivka

043 B

Architect: Anatolii Ihnashchenko
Artist: Anatolii Haidamaka,
with a team of approximately
80 executors (1979)
Smalt mosaic, relief,
stainless steel elements

The Literary Memorial Museum, established in honour of the Soviet writer of Ukrainian origin, Mykola Ostrovsky (in Russian transliteration – Nikolay Ostrovsky), is one of the most notorious institutions located in Ukraine. It was founded in 1946, on the 10th anniversary of Ostrovsky's death, in Shepetivka, where the author spent his childhood and adolescence. According to the current institutional myth of the founding of the museum, it was reopened in 1979 in this building designed by Ukrainian architects Mykola Husiev and Volodymyr Suslov. The construction took place near a monument to Ostrovsky, created by the sculptor Valentyn Znoba and the architect Ihor Lanko in 1966. Thus the structure, built on the money of the Komsomol organisation, formed the memorial complex dedicated to Ostrovsky.[34] The decoration of the building was conducted by a team consisting of approximately 80 artists. Two well-established Ukrainian artists were in charge of the group – the architect Anatolii Ihnashchenko and the artist Anatolii Haidamaka, both experienced in the creation of museums and memorial complexes. The mosaic on the circular part of the museum is truly extraordinary, not only because of its enormous square, which is covered with smalt chips (more expensive than ceramics), but also due to the fact that the facade of such an ideologically important building as this one lacks any image depicting the human form. The artists featured only the depiction of the red horse, commonly used as a reference to the October Revolution. The interpretation of the colour palette, embedded in the current representation of the museum's history, explains red as 'the struggle' and grey as 'difficulties in Ostrovsky's life'.[35] The most intriguing aspect of the cultural institution is the controversy revolving around the personality of Mykola Ostrovsky. In the context of the Soviet art sphere, it is truly ironic that the commemoration of the author of the book *How the Steel Was Tempered*, which altered the formation of the Socialist Realist literary canon, is visually performed in a way that harshly contrasts with 'the official method of Soviet art'. Additionally, the legacy of Ostrovsky was widely exploited in Soviet propaganda to combat Ukrainian nationalism. In particular, Ostrovsky is blamed for depicting the Army of the Ukrainian People's Republic (1917–1921) as cruel anti-Semites. However, the personnel of the museum insist on the opposite perspective on Ostrovsky. Basing their interpretation on archival materials from the 1990s, they argue that he was a victim of state propaganda. Currently, the author is included in the list of the individuals whose names should be excluded from the toponyms (the document was compiled by the Ukrainian Institute of National Remembrance).[36]

B

Horyn Hotel

11 Nezalezhnosti Avenue,
Netishyn

044 B

Oleksandr Yaremov,
Viktor Piontkovskyi, with the
assistance of Mykola Habruk
and Nadiia Yaremova
Prometheus (1983)
Smalt mosaic

Netishyn is a town in the Khmelnytskyi region, where the regional nuclear power plant is located. The preparation work for the plant's construction started in the middle of the 1970s, and the building was set up in the early 1980s. At the time the development of the town was considerably altered by the necessity to provide services and specialised personnel for the operation of the Khmelnytskyi Nuclear Power Plant. The Horyn hotel marked the beginning of residential construction. The case of the facade's decoration was marked as a 'top important task'. Initially, it was assigned to artists from Kyiv who pitched a project in metal plastics that was not accepted by the head of the nuclear power plant. Consequently, it was redirected to the local artist Oleksandr Yaremov, who prepared a sketch featuring the character Danko from Maxim Gorky's *Old Izergil*. According to the story, Danko ripped out his heart in order to enlighten the way for the people, lost in darkness. Despite the character's exploitation in Soviet culture as a symbol of self-sacrifice for the sake of the common people's interests, the sketch was not accepted by the regional art council. Then Yaremov altered Danko's figure by playing with his facial features – the beard and the frizzy hair – and Prometheus was born. For the creation of the panel, the artists and the executors used 5 tons of smalt of 27 colours, specially delivered from Lysychansk to Netishyn (smalt was produced in Kyiv and Lysychank at the local glass plants). The white blocks in the mosaic were compounded from the marble crumb, the leftovers from the construction of the hotel.[37]

Rivne Plant of High-Voltage Gear

16 Bila Street, Rivne

Unknown artist
Smalt mosaic

045 B

The artist exploited the contrast between the black and white depiction of workers and a background abounding in colour. The heroes are pictured in a manner which is close to graphic art. In placing of the panel, the artists took into account the architectural features of the facade, and the consideration of the blank space facilitated the construction of a balanced composition.

B

Lutsk Driving School of the Ukrainian Defense Society

046 B

46 Peremohy Avenue, Lutsk

Vasyl Hura (1970s)
Ceramic mosaic

The driving school in Lutsk is one of the oldest educational facilities of its type in Ukraine. Initially, it was an automobile and motorcycle club founded in 1948 under the supervision of a voluntary organisation that supported military development of the region. In 1975 it was restructured into the driving school of the regional Defense Society.[38] We suggest that the decoration of the facade, created by Vasyl Hura, the Head of Volyn Art Production Workshops in the 1970s, is linked to the restructuring of the club. The artist depicted male figures who are involved in activities commonly associated with military service. He preserved the ideological symbol of communism – the five-pointed red star – on the uniforms of the characters. However, the abstract background, compounded by the coloured geometric blocks, is an artistic solution strikingly distinct from the Socialist Realist aesthetic.

B

Bus stop Sugar Factory
18 Zavodska Street,
Volodymyr-Volynskyi

Unknown artist
Ceramic mosaic

047 B

The mosaic which decorates the bus stop is dedicated to the history of Volodymyr-Volynskyi. The inscription reminds us that the city was the centre of the region. The schematic depiction of the characters and the application of the fully coloured blocks in the composition are rather unusual features for Ukrainian monumental and decorative arts.

ЦУКРОВИЙ
ЗАВОД
ОТЪ ЛѢТА 1199 ВЛАДИМІРЪ БЪІЛЪ СТОЛЬНЪІМЪ ГРАДОМЪ ГАЛИЧА Г ВОЛИНІ

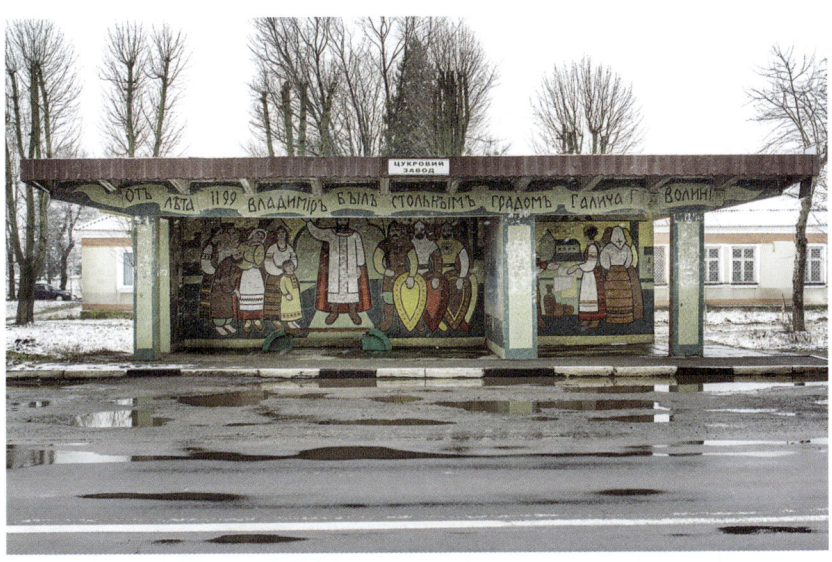

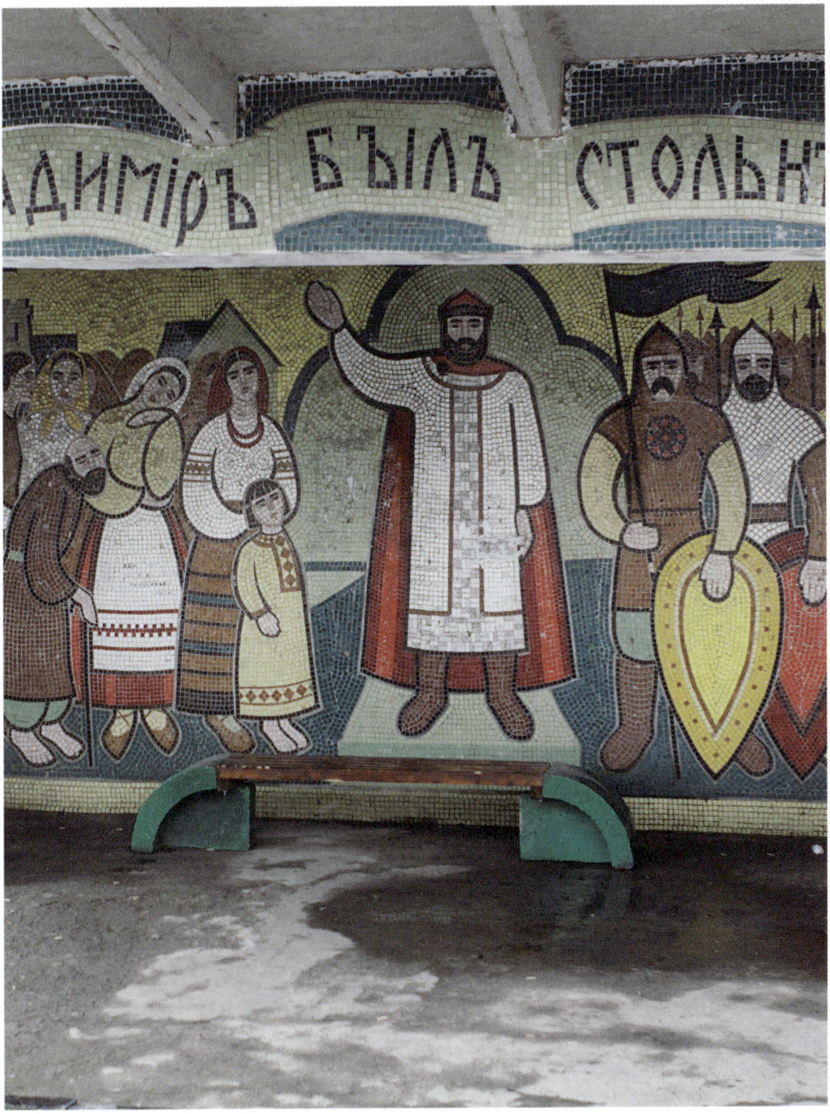
АДИМІРЪ БЪІЛЪ СТОЛЬН

Shakhtar House of Sport
3 Peremohy Avenue,
Novovolynsk

Unknown artist
Ceramic mosaic

048 B

The facade of the Shaktar House of Sport is decorated with a mosaic that utilises symbols uncommon to Soviet art. The characters are portrayed naked (the depiction of nude bodies was banned from Socialist Realism). The artists created the background with tinted curves to contrast the framework, the straight lines and the red accents on the young mens' bodies, conveying a sense of movement. This sense is intensified with the visual comparison of the youth with the swallows.

B

South

C

Odesa-Central Railway Station Service Point

2 Pryvokzalna Square, Odesa

049 C

I. Shenker, Ie. Shevelman,
Iu. Halperin, M. Chereshnia,
M. Matusevych (1967)
Ceramic mosaic

The original building of the Central Train Station in Odesa was erected in the 1880s. In 1944, it was destroyed by the invading German army. Reconstruction began in 1950, led by architect L. M. Chuprin. The new project, designed by Chuprin, shifted the building to the South and transformed the original form of the train station by adding a floor and a semi-basement. The reconstruction was done extraordinary quickly. The building opened on 12 July 1952. Several modernisation projects were held between 1963 and 1983.[39] The mosaic at the service point depicts the fishing and agrarian activities of the Odesa region (note the gendered division of labour reproduced in the artwork). The big fish, caught by one of the characters, refers to the natural bounty of the region. The artists used a restrained colour palette where the mosaic circles allowed them to balance the juxtaposition of distinctly figurative art and an abstract background. Remarkably, one of this piece's artists, Mykhailo Chereshnia, is famous for bright oil canvases with geometric shapes.

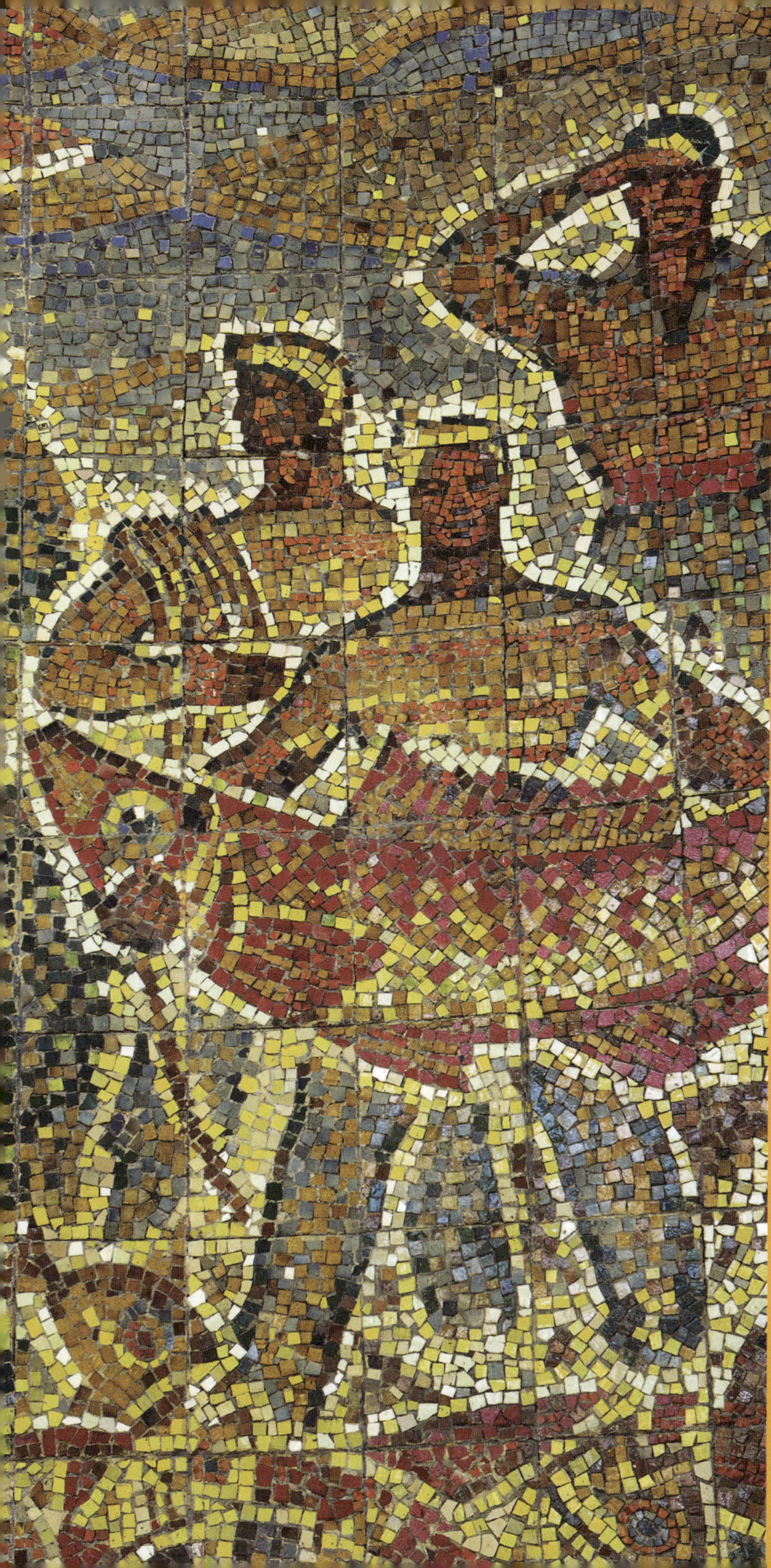

Comprehensive School no. 14
56a Krymska Street, Odesa

Volodymyr Tsiupko
Youth (1982)
Smalt mosaic

050 C

This artwork is created in a style that is clearly distinct from the requirements of Socialist Realism. The space of the panel is largely filled with tinted blocks; the primary accents are created with a bright red colour. The portraits of children, executed with the application of lines, merge with the background. One may note that the panel strikingly contrasts with the decorations of other children's spaces: it lacks any joyful and enthusiastic ambience and does not convey an ideological message.

C

Rus Recreational Centre
1 Shevchenko Street,
Bilhorod-Dnistrovskyi

051 C

Liudmyla Iastrieb
Tourists (1970s)
Ceramic mosaic

During the Thaw, the Soviet Union experienced a revival of international tourism, regulated with several Party resolutions from 1955, which allowed Soviet people to travel abroad and established the procedure of obtaining special visas for such purposes. In the same year, the new edition of the charter for the state travel agency Intourist, founded in 1929, provided grounds for the development of both inbound and outbound tourism in the Soviet Union. Remarkably, in Ukraine hotels were lacking: in the 1970s, Intourist owned buildings only in six cities, and that did not cover the flow of tourists (in

Kyiv and Yalta there was a need to double the number of hotels; the lack of space for temporary residence was also high in Lviv, Chernivtsi, Uzhhorod, Donetsk and Ternopil).[40] The scarce statistics may be informative on the general tendency: in 1967, Ukraine was visited by 127,000 tourists from 60 countries (more than 25 per cent from the general number of tourists in the Soviet Union; Kyiv, Odesa and Yalta occupied the third, the fourth and the sixth positions respectively in the all-union rating).[41] We may assume that the hotel in Bilhorod-Dnistrovskyi was built in order to satisfy the demand for residential spaces for tourists. The mosaic on the facade was created by Liudmyla Iastrieb, who combined the experiments of the avant-garde with motifs from Ukrainian folk art in her oeuvre. At the time, she was a leader of an informal art group in Odesa, the members of which established the creative association 'Mamai'.[42]

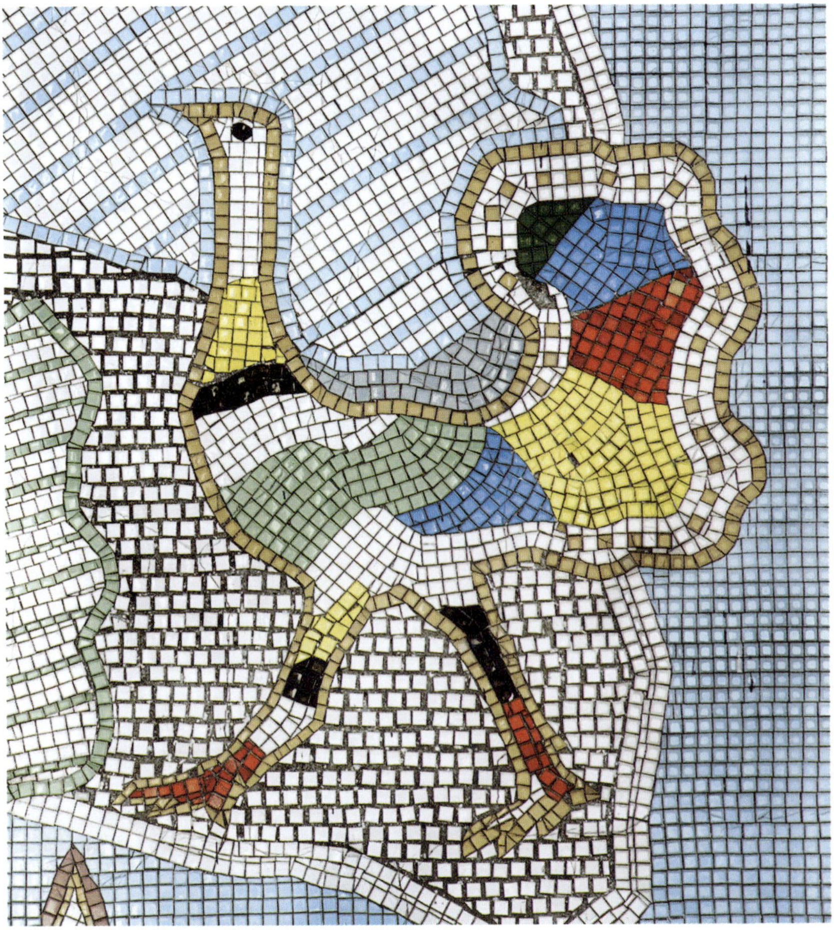

C

House of Culture
159 Kyshynivska Street,
Vypasne

Unknown artist
Ceramic mosaic

The facade of this house of culture represents primary subjects of Soviet monumental and decorative arts: nuclear and space programs, industry and agrarian activities. The approach the artists applied to the depiction allowed them to use the blank space of the facade as a structuring tool. The absence of any background intensifies the generalisations, encrypted in the figures: the characters appeal to each of the subjects as common personifications.

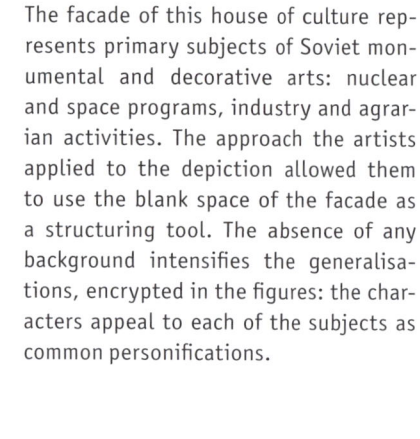

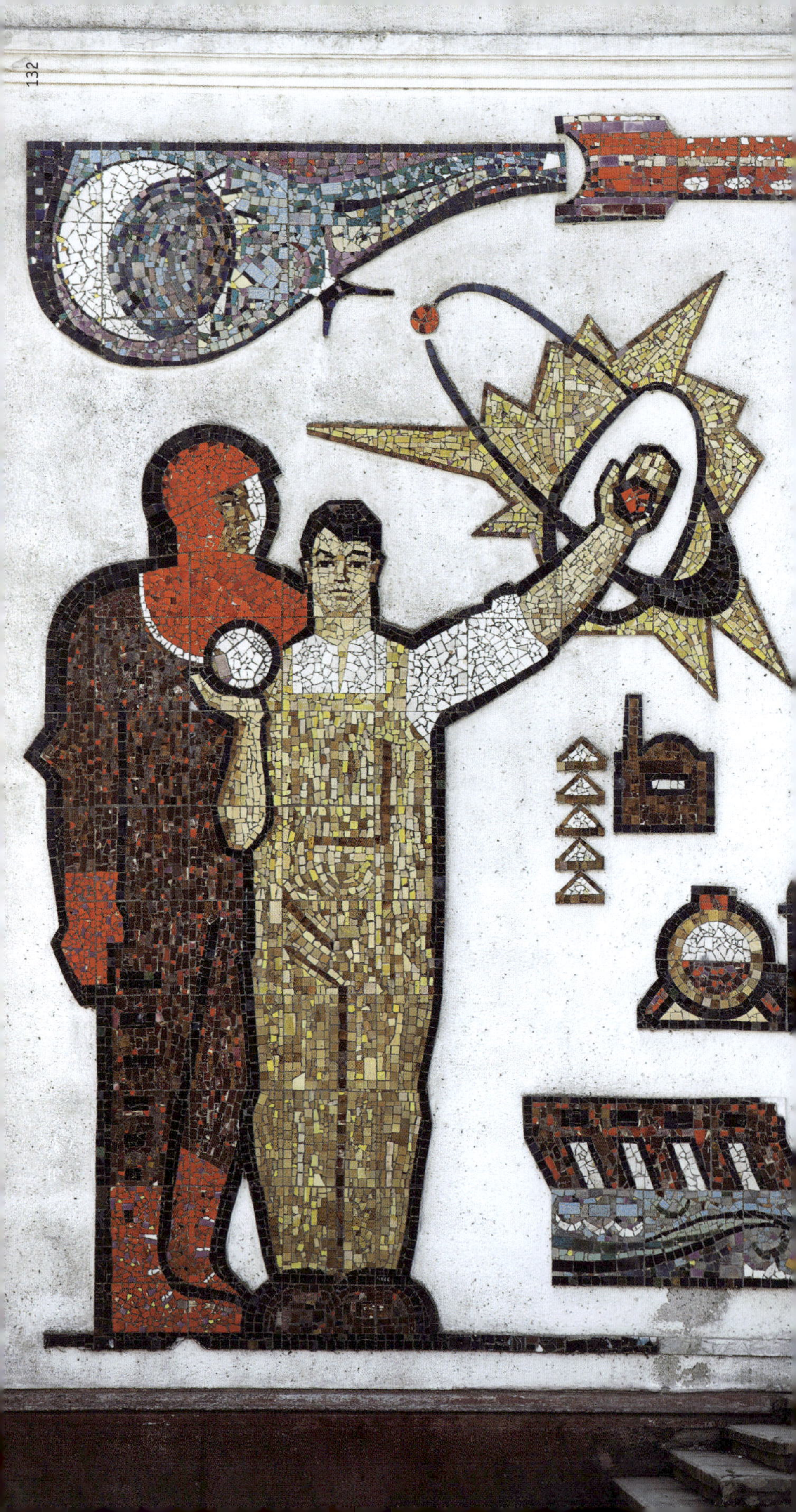

Gym and House of Culture
46 Semenova Street, Fontanka

Viktor Maryniuk
Sports (1980s)
Ceramic mosaic

The artist embraced the functions of the house of culture: one panel depicts characters involved in sports activities, another – dancers with an Ionic order column (a reference to Ancient Greek culture). The distinctive feature of the sport-panel lies in the artist's conscious decision to leave the faces of the athletes blank. It is a genuinely extraordinary trick in the context of the association of Soviet art with 'art of humanism', that spread in the 1970s.

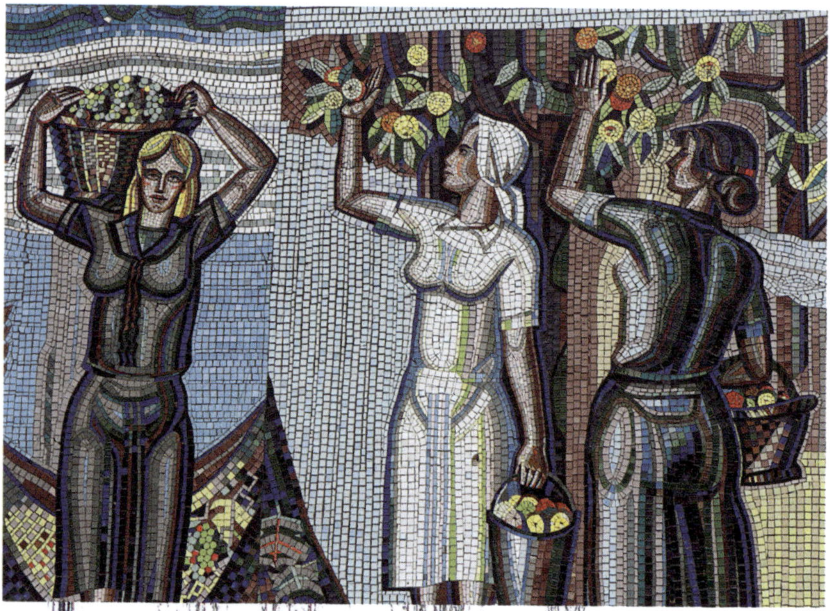

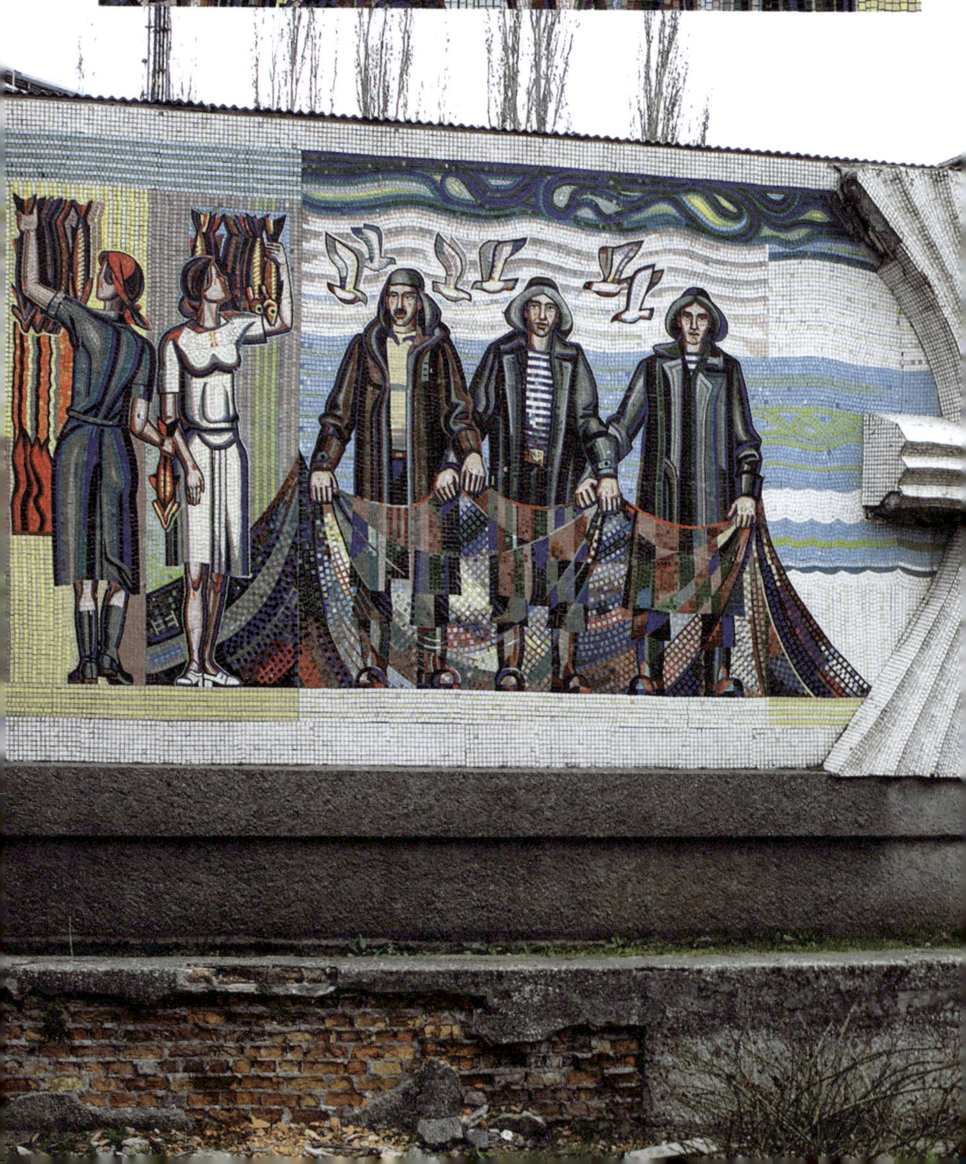

Department Store

2A Myru Street, Ochakiv

054 **C**

Mykola Berezhnyi
The Land of Winegrowers and Fishermen
(1970s)
Ceramic mosaic

Department stores from the 1920s were the institutions used by the Party for the promotion of mass retail.[43] A typical project of trading and household enterprises was developed by the Department of Typical Design of Kyivproekt in the late 1950s, together with the Institute of Structures of the Academy of Civil Engineering and Architecture of the Ukrainian SSR.[44] For the decoration of the facades of such buildings, it was generally recommended to use coloured concrete, ceramic or majolica inserts, but in practice, especially in the countryside, the choice of materials was very limited. In order to provide a building with 'architectural expressiveness', and for it to be noticeable in the landscape, artists often had to use intense colours in the decoration of the facades. That is not the case for the department store in Ochakiv; the colour palette is balanced and predominantly blue (Mykola Berezhnyi, the mosaic's creator, was a landscape painter). The subject of food production is portrayed through a historical linkage with the region's agrarian activities. The characters are depicted in harmony with their work, also a common image in Soviet visual culture, grounded in the idealised representation of a worker's daily life.

C

Shipbuilders Palace of Culture

3 Sudnobudivnykiv Square,
Mykolaiv

Volodymyr Bondarenko
(1972–1973)
Ceramic mosaic,
smalt mosaic

This colossal panel glorifies shipbuilders and presents the history of sailing. The artist depicted all the essential symbols used for the navigation, from ancient times through modernity. He also portrayed the characters who embody all the professions involved in shipping. The depiction of figures, majestic and exalted, is canonical to Soviet art.

C

Kherson College of Physical Education

2a Kalnyshevskoho Street, Kherson

056 C

Riuryk Brailov (1970s)
Ceramic mosaic, concrete relief

As it was already mentioned, the image of the young and sound body was one of the essential elements of the Party program for the 'upbringing of the Soviet citizen'. A strong physical culture was considered the means of such 'upbringing' and was promoted in all educational facilities. Nevertheless, in the 1960s, according to Mike O'Mahony, the subject of physical culture almost disappeared from the oeuvre of well-established Soviet artists, and it resurfaced in the 1970s in the critical artworks of the representatives of younger generations.[45] The construction of the college in Kherson may have been altered by the introduction of the new program with rigid standards placed by the All-Union Committee of Physical Culture in 1972.[46] At the time, the Soviet Olympic Committee also applied for the organisation of the Olympic Games in Moscow, thus the country needed to raise new athletes. Despite the fact that the mosaic on the college's facade conventionally depicts young sports persons, in terms of style it refers to abstract and geometric forms. The experience of Riuryk Brailov, who predominantly worked in graphics, has been translated here into the strict lines that resemble the linocut technique. One may note that this artwork lacks any Soviet symbols; this was uncommon for the approved sports sketches of the 1970s, when the subject was widely used to represent the Soviet Union internationally.

C

Oleshky Children and Youth Creativity Centre (the former House of Pioneers)

057 C

31 Hvardiiska Street, Oleshky

Unknown artist
Ceramic mosaic

The Houses of Pioneers exemplified the practical implementation of the notion that was particularly emphasised in the specialised press during the Thaw: children should have their separate space.[47] The modest and utilitarian building of the Pioneer Palace in Moscow, opened on the 1 June 1962 by Khrushchev himself, was considered as an important sign of 'destalinisation' in the architectural practice of the Soviet Union. During the Thaw, the Pioneer movement was separated from school education; places like the Houses of Pioneers were a means of structuring children's leisure in 'the proper socialist way'.[48] The buildings often comprised of spaces for distinct activities: home craft, aircraft modelling, arts, photography, science and technology. In small villages, their number was significantly limited due to available resources and personnel. The mosaics which cover the former House of Pioneers of Oleshky depict widely spread symbols of the Pioneer organisation – a banner, a bugle, a drum and a tie. The latter was a symbol of the involvement of each Pioneer in the affairs of the organisation, necessarily red, as well as the Pioneer banner. The mosaics also feature the face of Yuri Gagarin (who, by the way, was in the Komsomol organisation – the next stage of the Soviet youth development plan) and a depiction of the atom, both of which were embodiments of scientific enthusiasm, shaped by the Soviet space program and the construction of nuclear power plants.

**Nova Kakhovka College
Volodymyr Vernadsky Tavriia
National University**
1 Horkoho Street,
Nova Kakhovka

Unknown artist (1972)
Ceramic mosaic

058 C

These panels signify the unity of all people in the Soviet Union. One of the artworks tackles the variety of ethnic
groups who 'peacefully coexist[ed]' in
the country. Another one demonstrates
the association of science-based industry with agrarian activities, presenting
it as a successfully handled dichotomy.
The cosmonaut who personifies Soviet
space exploration is placed above terres-
trial solicitudes, representing the major
achievement of the Soviet people.

C

House of Culture
1 Torhova Street, Hornostaivka

059 C

Unknown artist (1973)
Ceramic mosaic

The panels in Hornostaivka embrace subjects frequently depicted at houses of culture. One artwork shows women and a man in Ukrainian national clothes. The latter holds a traditional musical instrument – a bandura. Another depicts the athletes, hinting at the active involvement of the Soviet Union in the international sports scene, as well as their desire to host the Olympics (represented by the torch). This mosaic generally celebrates the grace of Ukrainian culture.

C

C

House of Culture
7 Chornomorska Street,
Kalanchak

Unknown artist (1977)
Ceramic mosaic

060 C

This piece conveys the harmony in the daily life of the Soviet people in a way that is quite common in Soviet art. The artists portrayed optimistic characters, all engaged in work to increase the prosperity of the country. The family is centred in the composition, pictured with the background of an industrially-advanced city with greenery. The artists also referred to Ukrainian culture by depicting male figures with a bandura and a sopilka, Ukrainian folk musical instruments.

C

Gym of Dzhereltse Resort

68 Demisheva Street, Yevpatoria

061 C

H. Bondar, Iu. Bielkin
Smalt mosaic, ceramic mosaic,
natural stone

This panel is a notable artwork which employs Hutsul visual language. The artists used the natural stone as a primary material for the creation of the characters, and it defines the distinctive style of the object.

C

Bus stop Rezervne
Highway H19, Rezervne

062 C

Unknown artist
Ceramic mosaic

From the early 1960s, reconstruction and improvement of the highways in the country were emphasised at the state level for a range of reasons. Firstly, the restoration of highways was necessary for the logistical needs of industrial production. Secondly, well-equipped roads were considered an indicator of a developed country. And thirdly, the program of 'the aesthetic upbringing of a Soviet citizen', widespread from the 1960s on, contributed to the emergence of a new understanding of space that emphasised the organic unity of buildings within the surrounding landscape. This 'upbringing' ideologically stressed the aesthetic qualities of the human-created environment: decorated bus stops and regional boundary markings arose as new objects of monumental plastic art. This bus stop is in the village of Rezervne in the Sevastopol region. It was one of many inhabited localities in the area, renamed in 1945 after the deportation of Crimean Tatars initiated by Stalin. The previous name of the village was Kiuchiuk-Muskomiia (in Crimean Tatar – Küçük Muskomiya). The collocation has several interpretations, mostly because of the mixed roots of the second word. One of the interpretations suggests the translation 'Small Intermontane Region' (there was also the village of Büyük Muskomiya where 'büyük' means 'big'; its current name is Shyroke).[49] The creators of the mosaics on this bus stop depicted hills, particularly relevant in intermontane areas, with the animal inhabitants of the region – the red deer.

C

Miskhor Resort
9 Alupkinske Highway, Koreiz

Architect: H.Hvozdov
Ceramic mosaic, concrete relief

063 C

The Mishkor Resort is decorated with reliefs of imaginative forms and covered in ceramic mosaic. The artist carefully considered the placement of the object in the urban environment, so that the artwork would visually integrate with the landscape. The phantasmagorical reliefs clearly violate the requirement of realistic depiction intrinsic to Socialist Realism.

**Exhibition Hall at the
Union of Artists**
1 Hoholia Street, Yalta

064 C

Kateryna Zernova and Artists
of the Decorative Art Kombinat
Art (1967)
Ceramic mosaic, smalt mosaic

The construction of the Union of Artists building in Yalta was approved in 1967. The design of the hall was created by two architects, whose task, as Kateryna Zernova supposes in her memoirs, was to maximise the exhibition space with steady natural illumination. Zernova was assigned to the object by the Art Fund of the USSR.

According to her recollection, the artist was disappointed in the artistic requests from the representatives of the organisation. They were merely willing to depict still lives with the objects of decorative and applied arts (jugs, bowls, etc.) After wasting two or three months in torturing attempts to compose tableware, Zernova rejected the idea and concentrated on the people and nature of Crimea, which she could both comprehend and love. The sketches were not approved immediately: they were largely discussed at first, and after the Art Fund confirmed their execution, the Yalta Union of Artists reluctantly accepted them. The artwork was created in a workshop located in Vladykin

(Russia). Zernova notes that some of the executors were inexact and incompetent, and she did not have the opportunity to replace them due to the fact that there were no other specialists in the region. The installation was finished in 1968. The artist recalls that there was an issue with the tree image because smalt, as a material, does not exist in pink and lilac colours. Eventually, it was replaced with ceramic mosaic, transported to the location by Zernova's colleague, B. Kokorin.[50]

C

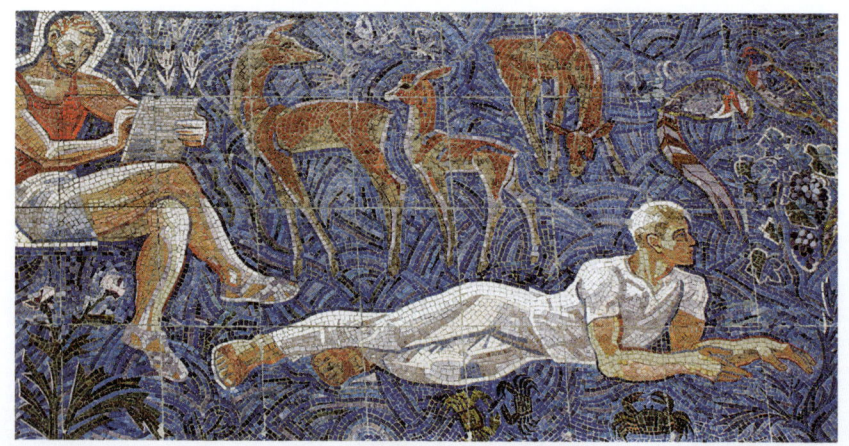

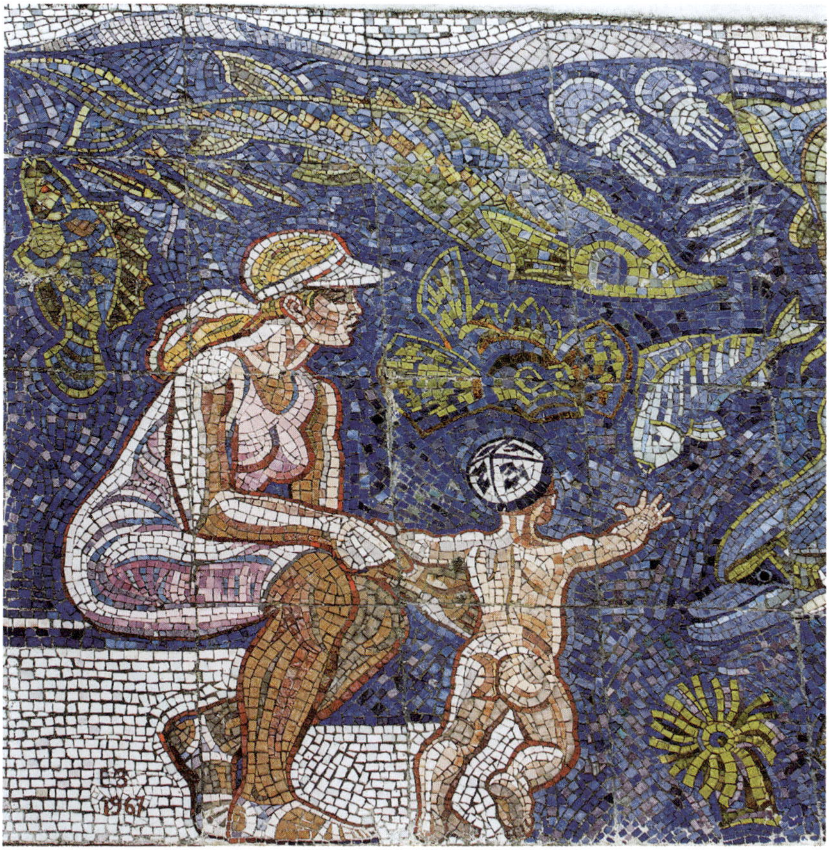
ЕЗ
1967

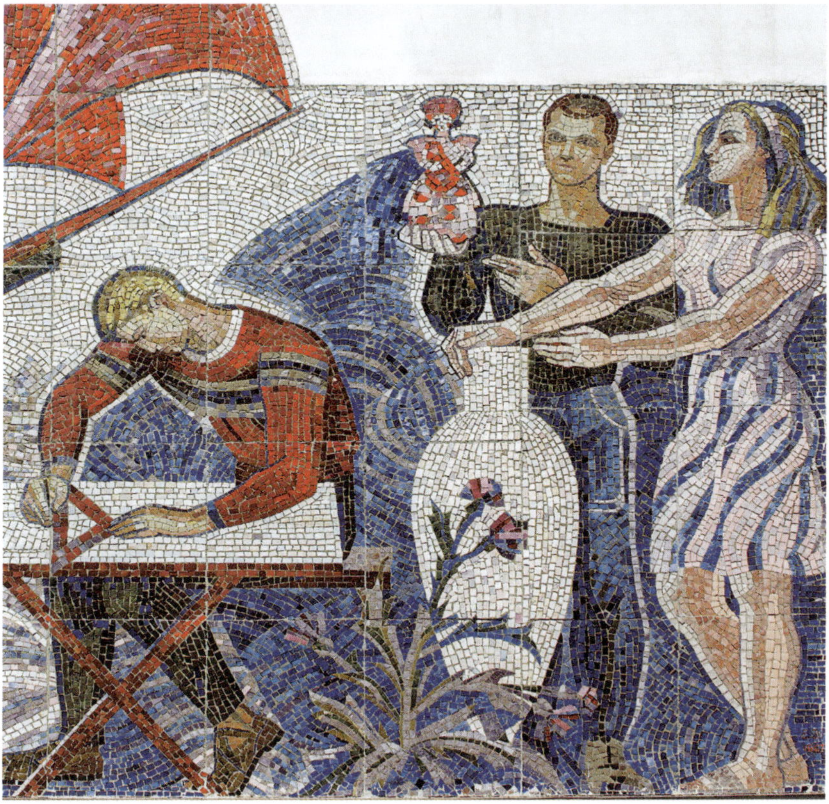

Zhovten House of Culture
20/1 Mykhaila Hrushevskogo
Street, Melitopol

Unknown artist
Ceramic mosaic, smalt mosaic

065 C

The artwork depicts a young boy with a bugle. The composition of the background is peculiarly structured with lines that define boundaries through distinct shades. Paired with a moderate colour palette where red, intensified with violet and blue, dominates the eye, it grants the artwork a unique rhythm and style.

Specialised School no. 25
93 Hetmanska Street, Melitopol

066 C

Olexander Fesiuk (1963)
Ceramic mosaic

The school is decorated with a mosaic that displays traditional subjects for children's spaces. A male and a female representative of the Pioneer movement gaze into the future, while the lower part of the panel describes their activities. The unique combination of day and night, the latter depicting various astronomical bodies, is an early reflection of the Soviet space program.

C

Children's Recreation Centre Red Carnation

1 Zaslonova Lane, Berdyansk

067 C

Yurii Andrushchenko
May There Always Be Sunshine (1974)
Ceramic mosaic, smalt mosaic

The Pioneer camp Red Carnation was built in 1971 and still operates as a summer camp for children. The Pioneer camps were the most important places for the Pioneer movement: there, rituals were realised, gaining symbolic meaning and power.[51] In particular, building a fire, and spending time around it while talking, playing or singing were essential Pioneer activities. The creator of the mosaics referred to the Soviet song, *May There Always Be Sunshine* (lyrics by Lev Oshanin, music by Arkadii Ostrovskyi), which became especially popular in the 1960s. It originated from a quatrain written by the four-year-old Kostya after he learned the meaning of the word 'always.' The poem was originally published in 1928 in an article on children's psychology, after which Korney Chukovskyi used it in the children's book, *From Two to Five*. During the Thaw, the song became a symbol for youthful outlook nourished in the Soviet Union.[52] Remarkably, the buildings of the camp are decorated with mosaics that are far from being Socialist Realist in terms of style. The artist employed tinted colour blocks as the primary means of constructing the composition. Additionally, he portrayed the characters through sharp geometric shapes, contradicting the realistic requirement of 'the official method'.

![Mosaic mural at the Children's Recreation Centre Red Carnation]

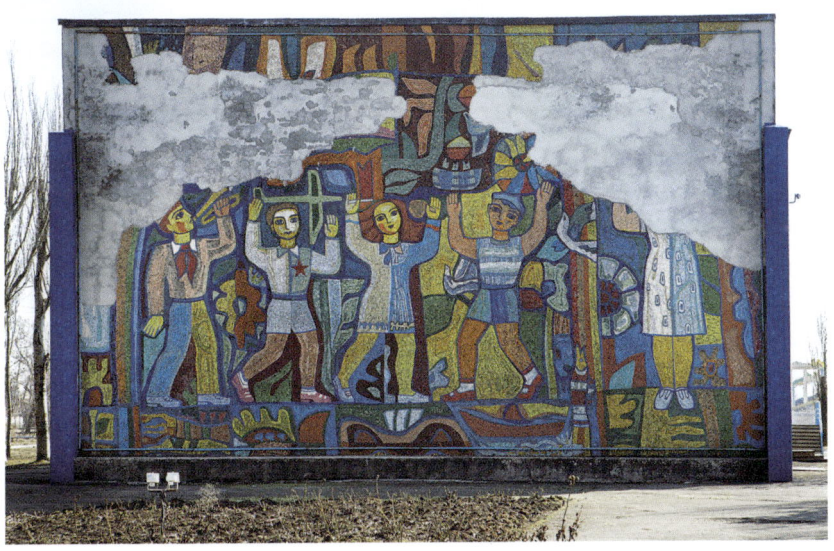

House of Culture
62 Tsentralna Street, Urzuf

Lel Kuzminkov,
Valentyn Konstantinov
Harvest Festival (1967)
Ceramic mosaic, smalt mosaic,
natural stone

068 C

Urzuf is a Greek settlement on the Sea of Azov. The subject of the mosaic refers to the decorative folk art of the Greeks who resided at the north coast of the sea (Pryazovia). The ornamental motifs and relevant colour combinations used in the piece are all common symbols of Greek folk art and design.

House of Culture

20 Gagarina Street, Melekine

Unknown artist
Ceramic mosaic, smalt mosaic

069 C

The village of Melekine was founded in the second half of the 19th century as a fishing artel, a pre-revolutionary cooperative of workers, and has remained as such for over 100 years. The mosaic refers to the history of the settlement, merging a realistic depiction of brave sailors with geometric elements that form an abstract composition. In addition, the stained glass windows have been preserved in the interiors of the building.

C

Comprehensive School no. 54 070 C
11 Kronshtadtska Street,
Mariupol

Victor Arnautoff,
Hryhorii Pryshedko (1965)
Ceramic mosaic

In the 1960s, in order to legitimise Khrushchev's power, a campaign for the separation of childhood activities was intensified. Within it, the need to segregate children in terms of architectural space was stressed. At the time, the articles on the equipment of children's corners appeared in the Soviet specialised press (and was particularly relevant for communal apartments).[53] Khrushchev's construction reform of 1955 implemented the development of a nationwide project for schools, considered 'important places of ideological upbringing'. In the early 1960s, a separate resolution of the Party and the Council of Ministers of the USSR 'On School Building and Means of Strengthening the Material Base of Schools' was adopted. In Ukraine, a series of typical school projects was developed by architects I. Karakis, S. Sova, N. Savchenko and T. Ter-Arutiuniants, on the basis of an experimental project of a school, located in Kyiv on the Boulevard of Druzhby Narodiv.[54] The mosaic decorating the comprehensive school no. 54 in Mariupol was created by Victor Arnautoff. His artistic career was a truly unique case in the Soviet Union. Between the late 1910s and the early 1920s, he emigrated to China, and then to the USA. From 1929 through 1931, the artist frequently visited Mexico where he studied monumental arts under the guidance of Diego Rivera. In the 1960s, after years of the professorship at various universities (including Stanford University), Arnautoff returned to the USSR, where he received citizenship.[55] In his oeuvre, one can easily trace a connection with Rivera's monumental artworks (exemplified in this mosaic, particularly in the shape of the sun). According to the recollection of Arnautoff, he aspired 'to create something unique, something light and joyous to reflect the happy childhood of pupils, their eagerness and their concerns' in the artwork.[56]

Azov Machine Building Plant, Workshop no. 138

071 C

1 Mashynobudivelnykiv Square, Mariupol

Lel Kuzminkov, Valentyn Konstantinov
Motherhood, Sports, Labour
Ceramic mosaic

One may encounter these mosaics while travelling from Donetsk to Mariupol: they are located in the area of the Azovmash Power Plant. Nowadays, access to them is restricted. Nevertheless, the piece is highly visible from the highway near the Stadium tram stop. Azovmash is the largest engineering enterprise in Ukraine. Initially, four mosaics were created on the walls of the workshop: *Maternity,* *Sports, Labour* and *Education*. Only two of them were preserved completely and one only partially. Additionally, we strongly recommend that you visit the Iskra Palace of Culture that belongs to the plant (located at Nikopolsky Boulevard, 145). The facade of the plant and its premises are similarly decorated with well-preserved mosaics, created in 1965 by the artists from Kyiv.

C

Aristocrat Restaurant
48 Myru Avenue, Mariupol

072 C

Viktor Zaretskyi, Alla Horska,
Halyna Zubchenko, Hryhorii Pryshedko,
Borys Plaksii with Vasyl Parakhin and
Nadiia Svitlychna
Boryviter/The Bird of Hellas (1967)
Smalt mosaic, slag glass ceramic,
ceramic tiles, aluminium

The mosaic decoration of the Aristocrat Restaurant was created by Ukrainian artists who are commonly associated with the generation of the 1960s (the Sixtiers, *shistdesiatnyky*), and who were also involved in the human rights movement. The Sixtiers participated in the research and promotion of Ukrainian culture and initiated the investigations into the crimes of the regime that were concealed by the authorities. Consequently, many of the artists were imprisoned, expelled from their creative unions and purged; their artworks were destroyed.

Alla Horska, the wife of Viktor Zaretskyi, was killed in 1970. This mosaic decoration was made by a group of friends – Alla, Viktor, Halyna and her husband Hryhorii, Borys and Nadiia, a philologist, who was invited by Horska (Alla helped her with financial and residential issues). According to the recollection of Plaksii, he remade the sketch of the monumental panel after it was approved. The artist changed the location of the artworks *Boryviter* and *Tree of Life* because he believed that the wall, windows and seascape are emotionally connected; this room should have depicted something that represents the force of nature (as the Bird of Hellas). The artistic group agreed with Plaksii's modification. The change resulted in a big scandal for the Artistic Council that approved the previous sketches, and for Alla Horska charged herself with it.[57] Currently, the restaurant is not open; however, you can ask the security officer, who is on guard there day and night, to show you the mosaics.

Alla Horska, Halyna Zubchenko,
Hryhorii Pryshedko, Borys Plaksii
Tree of Life (1967)
Smalt mosaic, slag glass ceramic,
ceramic tiles, aluminium

The artwork *Tree of Life* was also completed in 1967. Nevertheless, it was a part of the premises for only 13 years – in 1980 the panel was immured, to be reopened as recently as 2008. The artists used not only common smalt and ceramics but also slag glass and steel. The metallic elements are the leftovers from the local metallurgist industrial enterprise.

Mariupol Railway Station
74 Linnyka Street, Mariupol

073 C

Lel Kuzminkov,
Valentyn Konstantinov
Steelmakers (1975)
Smalt mosaic, marble, granite

The decoration of the hall of the railway station in Mariupol was created by the artists of Greek origin Kuzminkov and Konstantinov, old friends and colleagues that created monumental and decorative works together. In particular, their mosaics decorated the premises of the Azov Machine Building Plant, which specialised in the production of mining and metallurgical equipment. The artwork at the railway station, like many similar pieces created in the Soviet period, refers to the profession common in the region. However, in terms of style, the mosaic's composition is organised with the application of peculiar geometric forms. Kuzminkov and Konstantinov located the bright figures corresponding to a circular principle that allowed them to convey the dynamics of the scene. The artwork pictures the complete cycle of casting, which the artists observed in the plant premises while creating the sketches for the mosaic. The colour palette of the object with prevalent orange and red colours is also inspired by the daily work of steelworkers and reflects the inner appearance of the steel casting workshop.

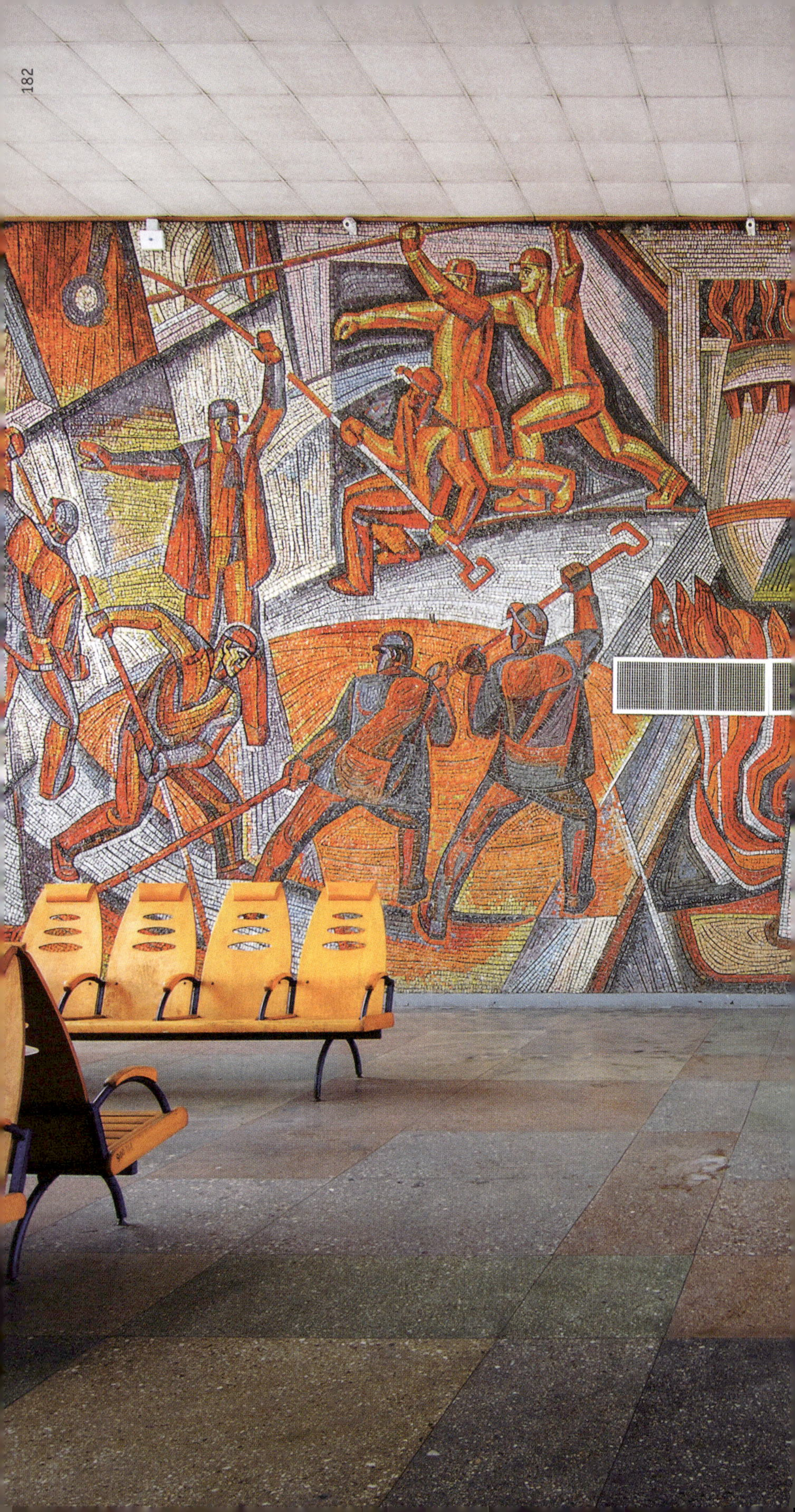

East

D

Ukraina Cinema and Concert Hall
35 Sumska Street, Kharkiv

074 D

Artists: E. Rohanova, V. Vasyliev
Architect: V. Vasyliev
Ukraine (1963)
Ceramic mosaic

The Ukraina Cinema and Concert Hall was built in 1963. The building embodies the aesthetics of Soviet modernism in the architectural landscape of Ukraine. The project was designed by the architects Vadym Vasyliev, Yurii Plaksiiev and Volodymyr Rieusov.[58] Vasyliev, who was also the designer of the Kharkivska-1 Water Pavilion in Sarzhyn Yar,[59] was an artist local to the Kharkiv region. Generally, architects took part in the creation of mosaics, predominantly as executors, due to the lack of specialists and the rigid deadlines of the orders. In these cases, they were defined as 'non-core' or 'secondary' workers. The artists depicted a woman with a lyre, the personification of Ukraine, over a background of the sun, the rays of which take over the entire space, connecting the yellow colour with the blue. As mentioned previously, this combination was vigorously censored in the monumental and decorative arts because it was associated with 'Ukrainian bourgeois nationalism'. The violet ceramic tiles, applied for garnishing of the building, was also used in the most famous constructivist object in Kharkiv – Derzhprom (or Gosprom) – which was the highest building in Europe at the time it was built in 1928.

D

КРАЇНА

Miskelektrotrans
Dormitory no. 2

075 D

98 Plekhanivska Street, Kharkiv

Vitalii Lenchyn
Development of Urban Electric Transport
(1972)
Ceramic mosaic

The mosaic on the facade of the dormitory reveals the history of the development of urban transportation. The piece stresses the 'progressiveness' of Soviet electric vehicles and the prominence of bringing them into public service. The artwork quite clearly conveys the ideological message of the technological superiority of the Soviet Union. Nevertheless, in the creation of the panel, the local artist Vitalii Lenchyn tended to a flat, schematic depiction, which he highlighted with the contrasting tinted blocks. Truly, his conception of art education was summarised by his students in one statement: 'Form is an organised space.' Within Lenchyn's pedagogical practice (which included teaching for distinct age groups, in a university environment and beyond), he insisted that the structure of space and form be constituted by the interconnection of vertical, horizontal and diagonal lines. The artist's views on art can be seen manifested in the execution of this mosaic.[60]

D

О СПОРТ! ТЫ – МИР!

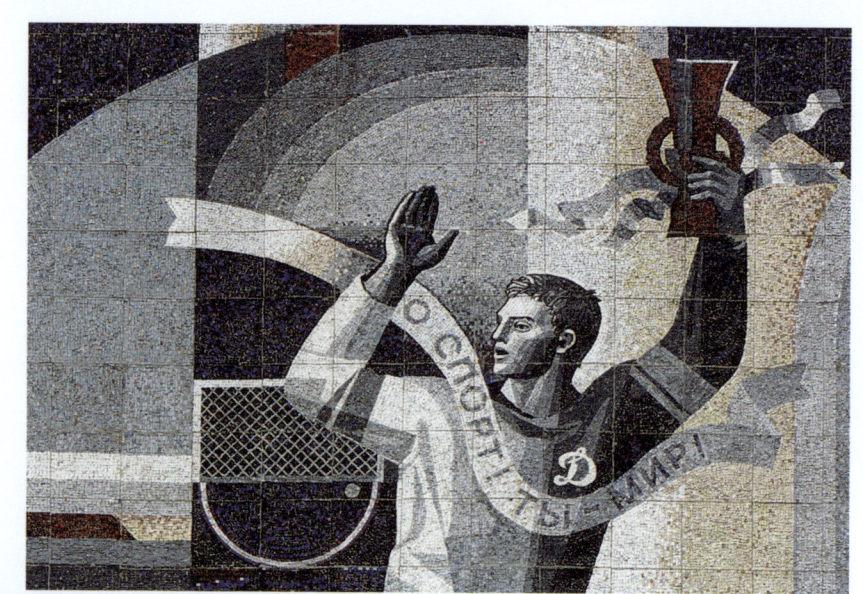

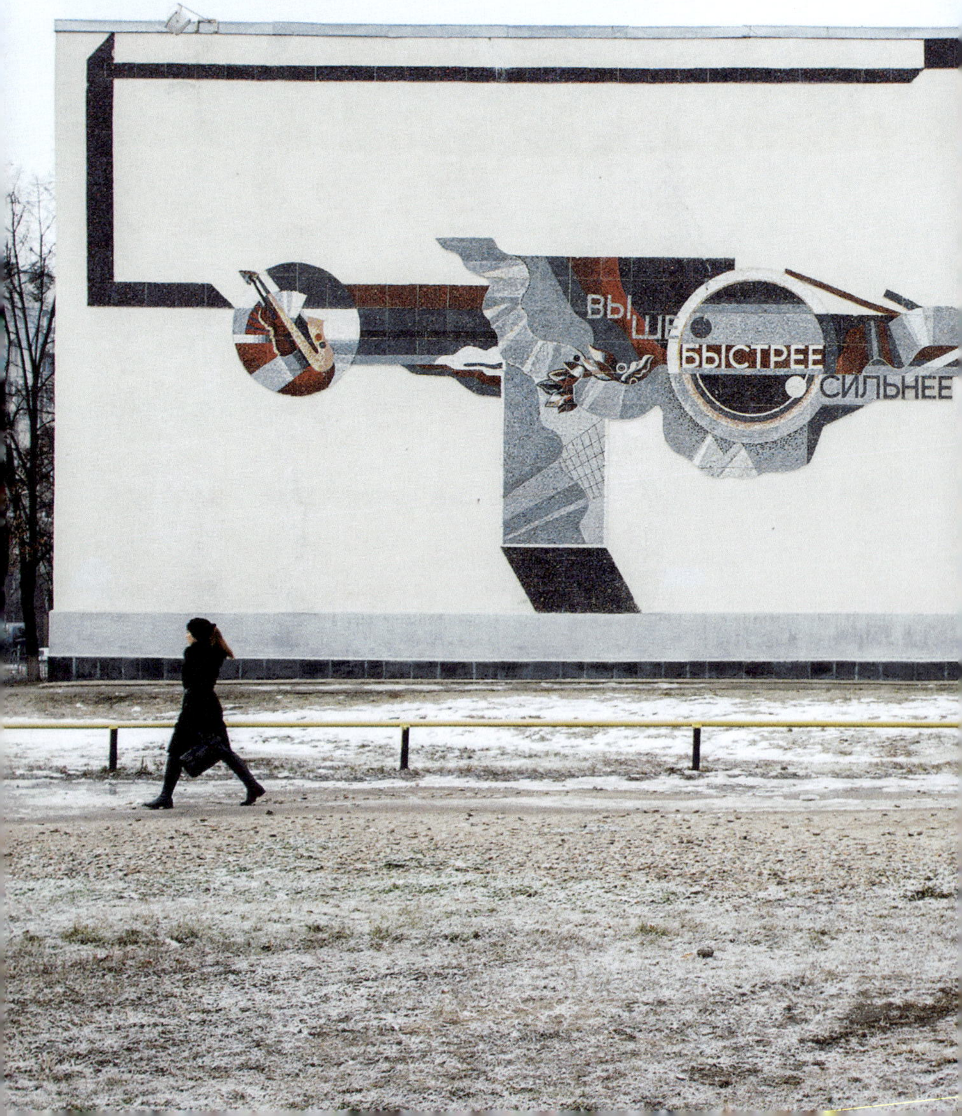
ВЫШЕ
БЫСТРЕЕ
СИЛЬНЕЕ

Kharkiv Palace of Sports

2 Petra Hryhorenka Avenue, Kharkiv

076 D

Unknown artist (1977)
Smalt mosaic

The mosaic was created in the late 1970s, before and in preparation of the Olympic Games of 1980 when the Soviet Union hosted the event. The Olympic-theme served as a primary reference for the creators of the decoration. The inscription 'O Sport, You are Peace!' carved on the strip and carried by a hockey player, is a quotation from *Ode to Sport* (1912), written by Pierre de Coubertin, the founder of the Olympic Games (initially published under the pseudonyms Georges Hohrod and M. Eschbach). In the Soviet Union, it became an easily recognisable phrase after 1981 and the release of Yuri Ozerov's documentary on the Olympic Games in Moscow, which appropriated Coubertin's line as its title. Another inscription in the artwork is 'Higher, Faster, Stronger', which is the translation of the Olympic motto 'Citius, Altius, Fortius!' from Latin, originally proposed by Coubertin. Leading up to the 1980 Summer Olympics, Kharkiv was one of the Ukrainian host cities of the Olympic flame.

D

Post Office (former Sporting Goods Store)

39 Nauky Avenue, Kharkiv

077 D

Vadym Vasyliev
Avant-garde (1970s)
Ceramic mosaic

This mosaic, created by Vadym Vasyliev, is a clear allusion to the constructivist experiments of the 1920s, when the art movement shared with the government the utopian and enthusiastic vision for a new society. At the time, the subject of sports was visualised in the extraordinary technique of photomontage (Gustav Klutsis, El Lissitzky) and developed particularly in the design of clothes by Varvara Stepanova, Nadezhda Lamanova, Natalia Kiseleva and Oleksandra Ekster.[61]

Vasyliev's mosaic is dedicated to the local football team, the Avant-garde Football Club (this name was used in 1949-1966; from 1967 until its dissolution, the club was known as Metalist). In the creation of the mosaic, Vasyliev was especially attentive to the sports costumes, worn by the figures. He depicted the uniform of the football team which was in use until the 1990s (after 1991 the white stripes were changed to yellow ones). The sportsmen form the line which stands for the collective nature of the sports; the pair of them look at each other, implying their support and care for each other during the game's activities. We suggest that because the authorities paid less attention to the decoration of insignificant buildings, the artist was able to gain approval of such a strikingly non-Socialist Realist sketch.

D

House of Culture
3 Tsentralna Street, Horodnie

Unknown artist
Ceramic mosaic,
smalt mosaic, relief

078 D

This mosaic truly lacks any ideological messaging as it does not employ any Soviet symbols or subjects. The artists applied an unusual approach: they depicted a table from an overhead perspective, and framed it with characters in Ukrainian national dress. The artwork conveys a joy for life in a manner vastly contrasting common Soviet images. It concentrates on the feast, featuring unregulated entertainment activities; in contrast to the ordered and emasculated 'harmony of daily life in the Soviet Union'.

Impuls House of Culture
37 Zavodska Street, Shostka

079 D

Unknown artist
Ceramic mosaic

The Impuls factory was a part of the Shostka Gunpowder Plant, founded approximately in 1771. The plant supplied the Russian army with weapons and various military equipment. After the October Revolution between 1924 and 1927, the factory had no operational plan approved by the state; it distributed products of mass consumption (food products, clothing, shoes, household items, etc.; so-called 'Group B' consumer goods). Shortly thereafter it was renamed – the Star Shostka Powder Plant. In the 1930s it was one of the first industrial enterprises to bring sulfate process technology into service. However, by the end of the decade many of its employees were purged, and operations were halted. 1940 and 1941 were an intensive period for the factory to produce military equipment.

In August 1941, together with the Svema Film Factory, the plant was relocated to Krasnoyarsk (Russia), and reconstructed two years later in Shostka. After the Second World War, gunpowder production decreased considerably; the plant supplemented the distribution of the products of mass consumption.[62] Impuls as a factory specialised in the production of explosive materials (such as blasting caps, electric detonators, detonating cords, etc.), was separated from the Shostka Powder Plant after 1848, and generally shared a similar fate in Soviet times. The houses of culture, as already mentioned, were the means of regulating workers' leisure. They were frequently established regionally under the supervision of local industrial enterprises. The mosaics decorating the facade of this building were obviously created after the launch of Sputnik. The authors touched upon common subjects in Soviet visual culture – sports and space conquest, exploiting the metaphor of construction appearing in Soviet art discourse in the 1930s.[63]

![Ceramic mosaic depicting figures with construction themes]

D

Residential Building
33 Zavodska Street, Shostka

Unknown artist
Smalt mosaic

080 D

The facade of this residential building in Shostka is decorated with a picturesque panel that resembles a watercolour painting. The flyaway red sails grasp the attention of the viewer. The sails may be a reference to *Scarlet Sails* (1923), written by the Russian author, Alexander

Grin, whose oeuvre was reintroduced during the Thaw. This ship and its red sails became the embodiment of the dedication to dreams and their fulfilment (for instance, Kateryna Zernova depicted the ship and sails on the facade of the Exhibition Hall at the Union of Artists in Yalta – see object 064). Nevertheless, the aircraft outline the presence of the demonstration of power in the artwork. This allusion may be linked to the Shostka Powder Plant. It shifts the focus of the object's narrative to a romanticised representation of the military.

D

Svema Swimming Pool
10 Shevchenko Street, Shostka

081 D

Unknown artist
Smalt mosaic

This swimming pool is decorated with an abstract composition that likely refers to the flow of coloured film, the main product of the Svema factory. The plant's name is an abbreviation from the Russian term *'svetochyvstvitelnye materialy'* ('photo-sensitive materials'). Svema was established on the basis of an agreement with the French film-making factory, Lumière, signed by the state on 1 September 1928. According to the agreement, the representatives of Lumière should have provided technical support in film production and necessary equipment. Due to the fact that the process of generation of nitrocellulose, the main component of film at the time, shared common features with the production of smokeless powder, the factory was built on the former premises of the Shostka Powder Plant. Svema opened in 1931 in the period of the rapid development of the Soviet cinema industry and produced various films and genres for the whole country. Remarkably, it is believed that the French consultants violated the agreement and did not provide any education on film production to the film-makers of the area. As a result, the local specialists had to develop their own methodology. In particular, the well-known movie by Fridrikh Ermler, *The Great Citizen* (1938), which facilitated the rehabilitation of Dmitri Shostakovich's compositional career – who, by the time, had fallen out of favour with the Party – was shot on film produced at Svema (it was the first Soviet movie, recorded on the Soviet film). During the Second World War, the factory composed aerial roll film, after the occupation it was transferred to Krasnoyarsk. In 1954 reconstructed Svema started to produce audiotape as well. During the Thaw, the factory also began to distribute amateur films that gathered amateur photographers and directors. Subsequently, they formed clubs for different ages which operated from 1970 into the 1980s. The members of the clubs cooperated with the local house of culture and specialised press, took part in amateur film festivals and even organised photo exhibitions. In 2019, while we wrote this book, Svema, declared bankrupt 15 years ago, was put up to auction with a quoted price of 13,500 euros.[64]

D

Water Tower
26 Mykolaivska Street,
Novhorod-Siverskyi

Ivan Loshakov
Lenin, Stalin (1937)
Ceramic mosaic, concrete,
natural stone

These mosaics on the water tower were created approximately in the 1930s. The artworks portray two leaders of the Soviet Union, whose images should have been destroyed according to the law 'On the Condemnation of the Communist and National Socialist (Nazi) Regimes, and Prohibition of Propaganda of Their Symbols', adopted in 2015 by the Verkhovna Rada with the initiative of the Ukrainian Institute of National Remembrance. Notably, the mosaics were not destroyed earlier, having survived the aftermath of the Secret Speech of Khrushchev in 1956, which launched the campaign of destalinisation.

Destalinisation was deployed in unsystematically in the sphere of visual arts: for instance, despite the fact that agenda of the First Congress of the Union of Soviet Artists in 1957 was altered – Soviets condemned the cult of personality – the Charter of the new Union exploited Stalin's quotation that Soviet art should be 'socialist in content' and 'national in form'. In Ukraine, the thematic plan of the most important exhibition dedicated to the 40th anniversary of the October Revolution still featured Stalin as a possible subject of artworks.[65] Remarkably, the mayor of Novhorod-Siverskyi considers the mosaics as local sights that have a potential to attract tourists; he even named it 'the Tower of Tyrants'. The mayor insists that it is impossible to transfer the mosaics to a museum without damaging the operations of the water tower (built in 1908) and asserts that, regardless of pressure from local activists and the Institute, the portraits will remain at the site.[66]

D

Faculty of Pedagogy and Psychology Oleksandr Dovzhenko Hlukhiv National Pedagogical University
25 Zelinskogo Street, Krolevets

083 D

Unknown artist
Smalt mosaic

As in many other countries around the world, football was extremely popular in the USSR and widely practised as a street game, as well as in state-funded semi-professional and professional contexts. Here, football players are portrayed as superhuman, moving quickly and force-fully in an abstract yellow and blue smalt cosmic sphere. The Olympic torch in the background refers to the Olympic Games, hosted in Moscow in 1980.

D

House of Culture

1 Myru Square, Krolevets

Unknown artist (1973)
Ceramic mosaic, smalt mosaic

084 D

This technically simple panel serves as an 'advertisement' for various activities people can enjoy after hours at the local house of culture. A controversial element here is the juxtaposition of 'high' and folk art, respectively represented by a cellist dressed in a tuxedo and a couple in national outfits. It illustrates a general Soviet tendency to present Ukrainian culture as exclusively folk and amateur.

D

House of Culture
59 Druzhby Street, Lyutenka

085 D

Unknown artist (1981)
Ceramic mosaic, smalt mosaic

This mosaic represents the advances Ukraine saw nationwide in the development of technology for the agricultural industry. The artists combined images of vehicles with a portrayal of women carrying a loaves of bread on towels, a Ukrainian symbol of hospitality. The roads around the village of Lyutenka quite poorly maintained, so we strongly recommend you follow this route: Krolevets, to Hadiach, to Lyutenka, to Lysivka to Reshetylivka.

D

Bus Stop Reshetylivka
Highway M03, Reshetylivka

Unknown artist
Ceramic mosaic

086 D

From the end of the 19th century, Reshetylivka was known for its weaving, carpet-making, and embroidery. There, folk arts existed in the form of home activities. However, in 1960, the weaving studios and the local artel were restructured into the Clara Zetkin Reshetylivka Plant. The employers of the factory workshops, including monumental artists, produced tapestries, carpets with floral and geometric ornaments, throw rugs, etc.

Bus Stop Machukhy
10 Frunze Street, Machukhy

Unknown artist
Ceramic mosaic, relief

087 D

For the decoration of this bus stop, the artists employed images of massive sunflowers to fill the majority of wall space. The peculiar feature of this piece is the execution of the leaves, for which the artists used relief and preserved the contrast in colouring.

D

МАЧУХИ

House of Culture
21 Myru Street, Snizhkiv

088 D

Unknown artist
Ceramic mosaic

Rural communities also experienced changes in their development, altered by the launching of the Typical Construction projects. The post-war period brought the necessity of rebuilding villages. In 1956, to cut expenses, the Party introduced a new regional classification: rural settlements in the USSR were deemed as 'promising' or not (the latter group included outposts with less than 200 people). As part of the Typical Construction plans and the 'promising' category, some villages were restructured into 'experimental and demonstrative rural communities'. Within the building of such towns, the government aspired to achieve the most convenient parameters for village construction, which was expected to be done by means of multistorey residential buildings. Generally in Ukraine, 'experimental and demonstrative rural communities' were built from scratch between 1965 and 1968, and many of the investments put into their construction commandeered support funds for other villages. In 1969 the Council of Ministers of the UkrSSR adopted a decree 'On Complex Experimental and Demonstrative Construction of Villages of Collective Farms and State Farms in the Ukrainian SSR' that manifested the Party's intention to build 41 villages as soon as possible. However, the plan was not realised due to enormous expenses – in the early 1980s there were only 19 'experimental and demonstrative rural communities' in Ukraine.[67]

D

Kramatorsk Museum of Fine Arts
60 Akademichna Street, Kramatorsk

Unknown artist
Ceramic mosaic

089 D

The life and work of industrial workers were among the most familiar images in Soviet monumental and decorative arts. Local branches of heavy industry defined which motifs might gain prominence in mosaic panels of any given region in Ukraine. This technically simple piece illustrates (in a sort of a comic strip manner) all stages of machine-building: from coal mining to iron smelting.

Comprehensive School no. 24

090 D

28 Bohdana Khmelnytskoho
Street, Kramatorsk

V. Rusiaiev, E.Rohanova (1962)
Ceramic mosaic

The comprehensive school in Kramatorsk was built in 1962 as a part of the experimental communities project, designed by the architect Yosyp Karakis and his former student Viktor Savchenko. It was one of the first advanced typical projects implemented in practice. In the mosaic, which marks the building's function in the general landscape, the artists focused on the pressing subjects of the time: sports and physical exercises, the Pioneer symbols (there were thirteen thousand Pioneers in the city in the early 1970s), the Soviet space and nuclear programs and the harmony of workers with their labour activities (note the conventional gender division). Despite the apparent ideological weight of the artwork, Rusiaiev and Rohanova separated each scene with geometric tinted blocks outlined with a darker colour; a rather original stylistic solution in the context of monumental and decorative arts.

D

Volodymyr Sosiura House of Culture

091 D

1 Heroiv Stalinhradu Street,
Lysychansk

Vartan Arakelov
Space Conquerors (1968)
Smalt mosaic

The Volodymyr Sosiura House of Culture is a former recreational centre of the Lysychansk Glass Plant (which provided the whole country with tiles and smalt). The house of culture was opened in 1966 along with wellness facilities at the glass and soda factories. The services provided there included physiotherapy, mud treatment, stink damp, carbon dioxide and other baths. The mosaics decorating the facades of the former recreational centre were created by Vartan Arakelov, the Soviet artist famous for his portrait of Stalin, executed in the technique of Florentine (semi-precious stones put together in such a way that the gaps between them are almost invisible). This image of Stalin was placed against the newly founded planetarium in Volgograd, formerly Stalingrad (Russia). During the destalinisation campaign, the portrait was concealed by the employees of the planetarium and restored in the 1990s. Experienced in the sphere of political poster, Arakelov created many recognisable Socialist Realist images of the Soviet leaders and cosmonauts, which in monumental and decorative arts, with their unique artistic style, look a bit droll. Remarkably, riding a wave of the Soviet space enthusiasm, the artist depicted Valentina Tereshkova in the centre of the mosaic composition. In 2017, another mosaic on the facade of the house of culture, *Always with Lenin*, was covered with the banner, bearing the inscription 'Love Ukraine', as a part of the implementation of the so-called 'decommunisation law.'

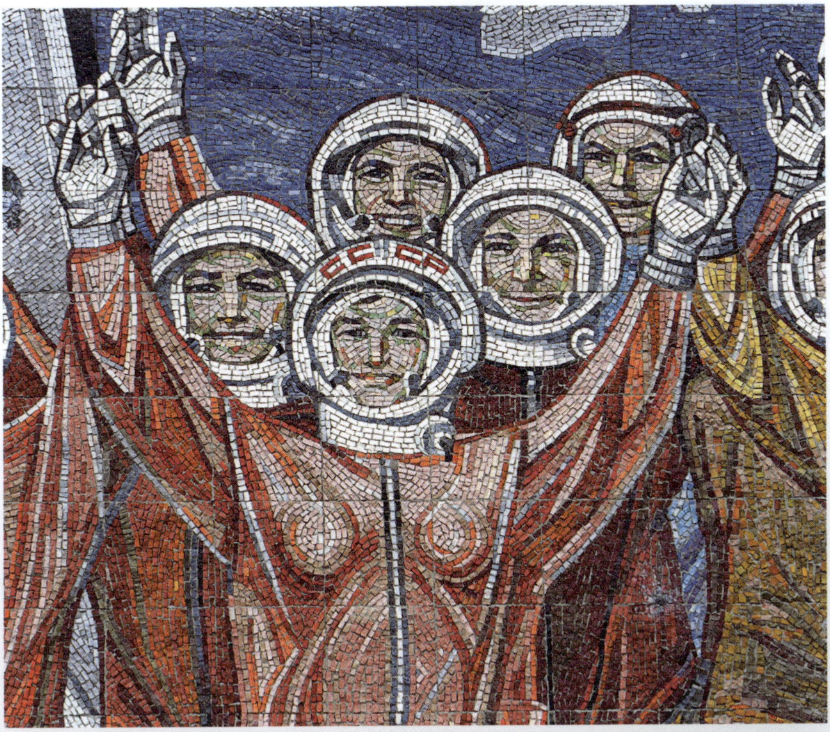

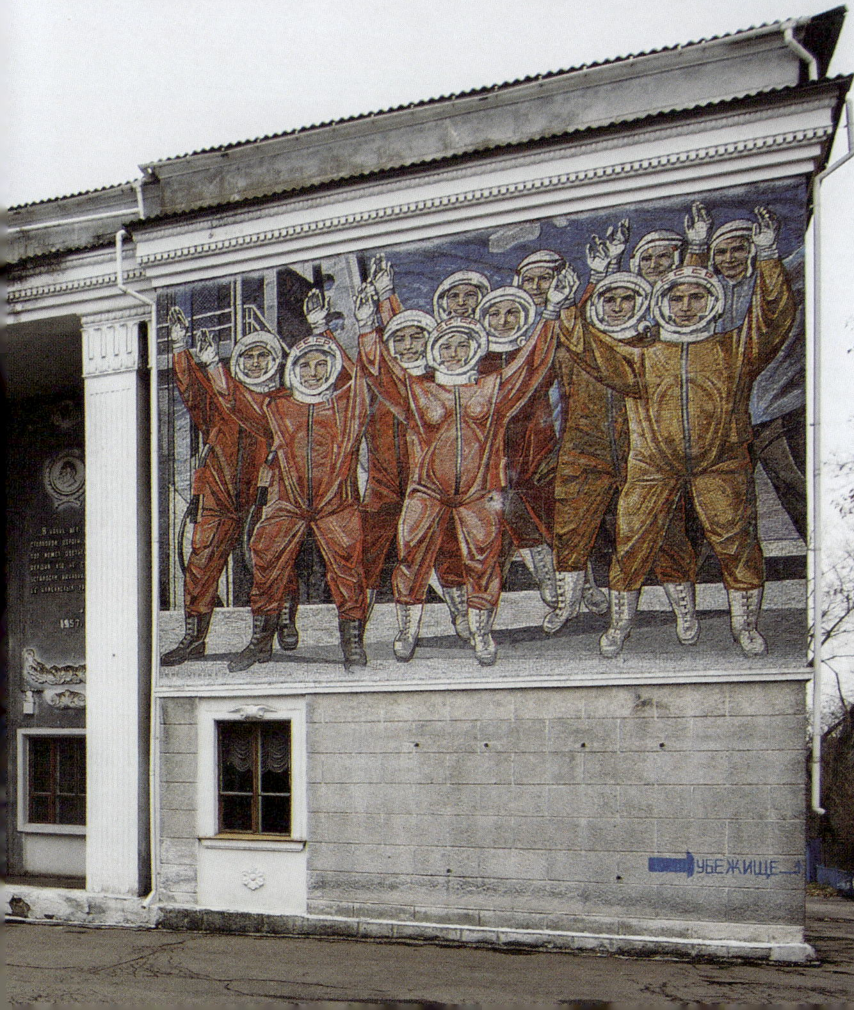
УБЕЖИЩЕ

Commercial Bank (former Zhovtnevyi Cinema)

3 Oleksandra Dovzhenka Street, Lysychansk

Unknown artist (1960s)
Ceramic mosaic

092 D

In this multi-figure composition, we would like to highlight the person who holds the coal in their hands. The discovery of coal in the Donbas during the 1720s is associated with the geologist Hryhorii Kapustin. The expedition, led by Kapustin, was the first one to reveal deposits of coal in the area of modern Lysychansk. Consequently, the history of the region has been shaped almost entirely by the discovery of the coal basin.

![Ceramic mosaic depicting a multi-figure composition in red, yellow, blue and white tones]

Ice Palace
28 Mayakovskoho Street,
Siverodonetsk

Artists of Siverodonetsk
Art Kombinat (1974)
Smalt mosaic

093 D

These simple yet elegant panels, executed in two major colour schemes (referring to cold and warm seasons), show various sports activities. The long chain of sport halls and massive state promotion of 'healthy way of living' made their impact on Soviet society. Along with football or jogging, many Olympic sports became trendy hobbies for people of all ages.

D

South Microdistrict Palace of Culture

11 Chekhova Street, Rubizhne

094 D

Mykola Uhrium (1970s)
Ceramic mosaic

A typical pre-modernist building of a house of culture, this structure was decorated with mosaic panels probably after its construction in 1961. Two symmetrical parts illustrate gender stereotypes, common for Soviet mass culture. Women, all dressed-up in a traditional outfit, two of them barefoot, are busy with leisure and household activities. While men are occupied with matters of state importance, such as atomic energy, chemistry, industry and military service. The kneeling figure clearly refers to the sculptural model of an Unknown Soldier, a prototype of simple, mass-produced monuments commemorating the Second World War and found in every small town or village. The static composition of this piece illustrates the aesthetics of Soviet propagandistic posters rather than the aesthetics of monumental and decorative arts.

D

D

Palace of Sports
100 Bohdana Khmelnytskoho
Street, Rubizhne

Unknown artist
Ceramic mosaic

095 D

The facade of this palace of sports, built
in 1971 in Rubizhne, is decorated with
an exceptional mosaic in the context of
Soviet visual culture. It depicts various
sports through characters created exclusively with black outlines. The background

is composed of chaotically placed spots of intense blue and yellow – a 'dangerous' colour combination due to its direct association with 'Ukrainian bourgeois nationalism'. The fingers of the central figure, as well as a ball, are executed as a relief, and doubled with yellow mosaic chips in order to convey the dynamics of the athlete's movement. The red circles, arranged in a row, emphasise the general composition and link the central characters with their contours, located below.

Palace of Sports Swimming Pool

096 D

100 Bohdana Khmelnytskoho Street, Rubizhne

Unknown artist
Ceramic mosaic, smalt mosaic

The premises of the former swimming pool at the palace of sports in Rubizhne is decorated with a mosaic executed in a manner distinct from that used for the panel on the facade. It depicts a male figure with sea inhabitants in space surrounded by various constellations. The horned moon frames the general composition from the left side. The symbolism of this particular artwork is difficult to decipher without any clues. However, the mosaic resonates with tendencies of the 1970s, when Socialist Realism was defined as an 'art of humanism' where, in contrast to Western modernist tendencies, the human was put in the centre of the artistic efforts. At the time, the oeuvre of Renaissance masters, which may have served as a reference for the male figure in the mosaic, was considered the origin of Soviet art. The notable feature of the piece is the nudity of the main character, something hardly tolerated in Soviet visual arts. The mosaic is located behind the locked doors of the non-operating swimming pool. However, the security guard will be probably glad to show you the remnants of long-faded grandeur of the interior.

Experimental School no. 5

097 D

5 Shkilnyi Boulevard, Donetsk

Viktor Zaretskyi,
Hryhorii Synytsia, Hennadii Marchenko,
Halyna Zubchenko, Alla Horska
*Prometheuses, Air, Sun, Subsoils, Life,
Earth, Fire, Water, Space, Man, Woman,
Bird Woman* (1966)
Ceramic mosaic, smalt mosaic,
relief, glass shards

Manual labour was often glamorised by the inclusion of decorative elements into its depiction, elements which grant this panel a slightly surreal ambience: the sparks of fire bloom into magic flowers. Here, two working-class heroes (a coal miner and a factory worker) are compared to Prometheus – a Titan from Greek mythology. He was credited with bringing fire to people and thus enabling progress and civilisation. The piece is made by one of the most influential artistic groups of the time, led by Alla Horska. Significant features of their monumental artworks involve coloured flamboyance and surreal elements, alienated from Socialist Realist art.

D

Moloda Hvardiia (The Young Guard) Museum

6 Komsomolska Street, Sorokyne

098 D

Alla Horska, Viktor Zaretskyi, Borys Plaksii
Architect: Volodymyr Smirnov
Relay Race / Banner of Victory (1969)
Smalt mosaic, glass shards, steel, aluminium

The mosaic decorating the interior of the museum in Krasnodon (currently Sorokyne), as well as the exposition of the cultural institution, is dedicated to the youth organisation, Moloda Hvardia (the Young Guard), which played a prominent role in the underground resistance during the German occupation of the area. According to the Soviet historiography, the members of the Young Guard distributed anti-Nazi leaflets and organised sabotage actions. At the beginning of 1943, the organisation was uncovered by the Germans and the majority of its members were killed, their dead bodies were thrown away in the mining tunnel. In the creation of this mosaic, the artists referred to a particular violent episode, known mainly from Alexandr Fadeyev's novel, *The Young Guard,* and Sergei Gerasimov's film based on the literary work. The scene altered the prevalence of red in the background of the mosaic. In the left corner, the artists pictured blue and beige corpses, embraced by flames. One of the figures, caught up in the moment of the downfall, links the scene to the central characters. From the viewer's perspective, the men and the woman, jointly forming the nucleus of the composition, are radiating. Such an effect, as Lizaveta German points out, is achieved by a special method of the65 smalt laying, derived from the practice of Byzantine masters. The second title of the mosaic, *Relay Race,* provokes a compelling interpretation, within which the central characters are considered to be the Sixties, or people involved in culture and politics in the 1950s and 1960s, descendants of the Young Guard who were inspired by the glorifying stories about the young partisans learnt in childhood and adolescence.[68] Currently, Sorokyne is located in the non-government controlled area of the Luhansk region, which since 2014 has been occupied by military units of separatists, guided and supported by the Russian state.

Centre

E

Dnipro-Lotsmanska Railway Station

099 E

22 Lotsmanskyi descent, Dnipro

Roman Shusterman, Leonid Talskyi
(1975)
Ceramic mosaic

As early as 1929, the Lotsmanska Railway Station was built at this site in Dnipro. The title was derived from the name of the village, Lotsmanska Kamianka, the settlement of the Cossacks who were sailing masters (*lotsmany*). The area of Lotsmanska Kamianka was merged with Dnipro when the railway station was built. In 1975 the station was restructured according to the project of the architect Yevsei Sorin and renamed to the South Railway Station (trains departed to the south). In 2017 it was given a new name once more – the Dnipro-Lotsmanska Station. The mosaic at the hall of the station depicts steel-workers, construction workers and scientists all working together for the prosperity of the industrial city. The characters are designed in a moderate colour palette. This artistic solution allowed yet-to-be-identified artists to accentuate figures through an intense colour contrast with the abstract and very vibrant background. This visual distinction stays consistent throughout the different styles in the framework and the characters. Sharp tinted stripes of various thickness, deepened with chiaroscuros, form the figures, while the background is put together with geometric and wavy patterns.

Slavutych Sport Complex

27 6th Strilkovoi Dyvizii Street, Dnipro

100 **E**

Roman Shusterman (1970)
Ceramic mosaic, smalt mosaic

'We believe in sports heroes. We need victories like we need air to breathe. We want to give all the records our resonant names', goes the refrain of the popular Soviet song *Sport Heroes*. Sport and a healthy lifestyle were a crucial part of the image of a Soviet citizen. Mosaic depictions of athletes were more stylised and free than those of workers or soldiers.

E

Suputnyk Cinema

18 Tytova Street, Dnipro

101 E

A. Sapelkin, L. Talskyi,
I. Ostapenko
Conquering Space (1962)
Ceramic mosaic, concrete, aluminium

The enthusiasm driven by the launch of Sputnik and the further development of the Soviet space program was embodied in the construction of cinemas with 'space names' and pertinent visual aesthetics: for example, Kosmos in Zhytomyr or Suputnyk in Dnipro. The latter was built for the Yuzhny Machine Building Plant, which produced rocket and space equipment. The construction was conducted in correspondence with the Typical Construction project, designed by the architects I.D. Mykhailenko and E.I. Sobol. Suputnyk Cinema opened on 15 May 1963. The dwelling initially included a variation of *cour d'honneur* (the yard in front of the building). The cinema accommodated 820 seats for spectators. Its facade is decorated with this large mosaic panel with washy colours. The artwork portrays the male figure, holding the hammer and sickle in one hand, while yielding an Earth satellite with the other. In the left corner, we believe the team responsible for the satellite's construction and launch is depicted. The artists used geometric outlines as the essential means of creating the image. The chosen style considerably limited them in the characters' design: some of the figures below are hard to distinguish, they resemble shadows. Additionally, the artists supplemented the panel with concrete and aluminium blocks that protrude from the building. Such a decision allowed them to draw attention to the satellite and convey a strong dynamism through the play with distinct planes. The cinema was shut down in 2009 and transferred to the supervision of a local ensemble. Its participants reconstructed the building on their own, and currently, the former Suputnyk operates as a concert hall where the local citizens celebrate weddings, children's birthdays and other festivities.

E

Meteor Ice Sports Palace

102 E

27A Makarova Street, Dnipro

Artist: Ernest Kotkov
Architects: Iurii Khudiakov,
Viktor Sudorhin
Meteorite (1983)
Smalt mosaic, marble, stainless steel

Meteorite is a piece from Ernest Kotkov's later works, created jointly with the architects Iurii Khudiakov and Viktor Sudorhin. The sculpture is more than 15 metres high, composed of stainless steel and concrete, covered in smalt mosaics. The artists completely neglected any connection with architecture, making the scene for the artwork out of the urban environment. Kotkov, Khudiakov and Sudorhin redefined the position of monuments and mosaics, reaching for a 'synthesis of arts' beyond the flat spaces of architectural exteriors. For the creation of the object, the artists, presumably, used a modified method which was initially applied by Kotkov's colleagues, Lytovchenko and Priadka in the artwork *Sun of Love*: the stationary construction of twisted metal rods was filled with aerated concrete, covered with a two-centimetre layer of concrete, painted with tempera and then covered with mosaics.[69]

E

Pavlohrad Unit of Ukrtelecom
58 Soborna Street, Pavlohrad

103 E

Unknown artist
Ceramic mosaic

The mosaic panel on the facade of the Unit of Ukrtelecom widely refers to the history of Pavlohrad. After the Second World War, the city became famous for its underground resistance movement against Nazi invaders, organised by local citizens. It is believed that the partisans (resistance fighters) sabotaged the operation of local industrial enterprises, disrupted the communication between German command centres, exploded bridges which connected the settlements and even obstructed the functioning of the railway station. Eventually, the resistance organised an armed revolt that helped the Red Army to liberate the area. The story about the partisans became a significant part of the Pavlohrad's narrative, thus the artists featured the military men in the left corner of the artwork. During the Thaw, the city became the centre of the charcoal industry in the Dnipro region, and, in accord with the Party's aspiration to a scientific approach in the governing of society, it became the location for various research institutions. Consequently, the creators of the mosaic emphasised the unity of the scientists and miners in the framework of the mosaic. In the centre of the composition, the artists placed the heroic image of strong characters (probably, communication workers).

E

Fire and Rescue Service no. 7
5 Vasylia Serhiienka Street,
Zaporizhzhia

Volodymyr Khomchyk (1986)
Smalt mosaic

104 E

The panel depicts an athletic male figure in a fireman's uniform with a fire horn in his hand, running towards the source of an open fire. In the background, one can see the outlines of a dam, a part of the Dnieper Hydroelectric Station – the largest hydroelectric power station on the Dnieper River – located in Zaporizhzhia. On the right side, there are several flags, one of which is decorated with a recognisable Cyrillic 'D' letter – a coat of arms for Dynamo Sports Society.

Zaporizhzhia Central Post Office

133 Sobornyi Avenue, Zaporizhzhia

105 **E**

Unknown artist (1967)
Smalt mosaic

The mosaic panel on the facade of the Central Post Office in Zaporizhzhia seems to refer to the local water power plant that defined the development of the city in the 20th century. The Dnieper Hydroelectric Station was conceived already in the early 1920s, when the preparatory studies and arrangement works were conducted. Between 1923 and 1926, because rifts in the soil were widespread throughout the water, the government launched the construction of Oleksandrivska Dam which revived ship-movement in the region. In the late 1920s, the hydroelectric power station

was built and the electric network was established. The construction of the dam was led by the Russian engineer Ivan Aleksandrov, who also was in charge of the special organisation, Dneprostroi. In 1929, the project design of the station, developed by a group of architects led by Viktor Vesnin, won an architectural competition (Vesnin also took part in the restoration of Zaporizhzhia after the Second World War). The construction of the power plant had an official consultation by the American engineer Hugh Cooper. The Dnieper Hydroelectric Station was opened on 1 October 1932.[70] Up to the present day, it remains one of the essential sources of electricity for the region. Therefore, the creators of the mosaics depicted the power plant by exploiting the same symbolism as is in the artwork dedicated to Prometheus: bringing light to common people by the extraordinary efforts of individuals.

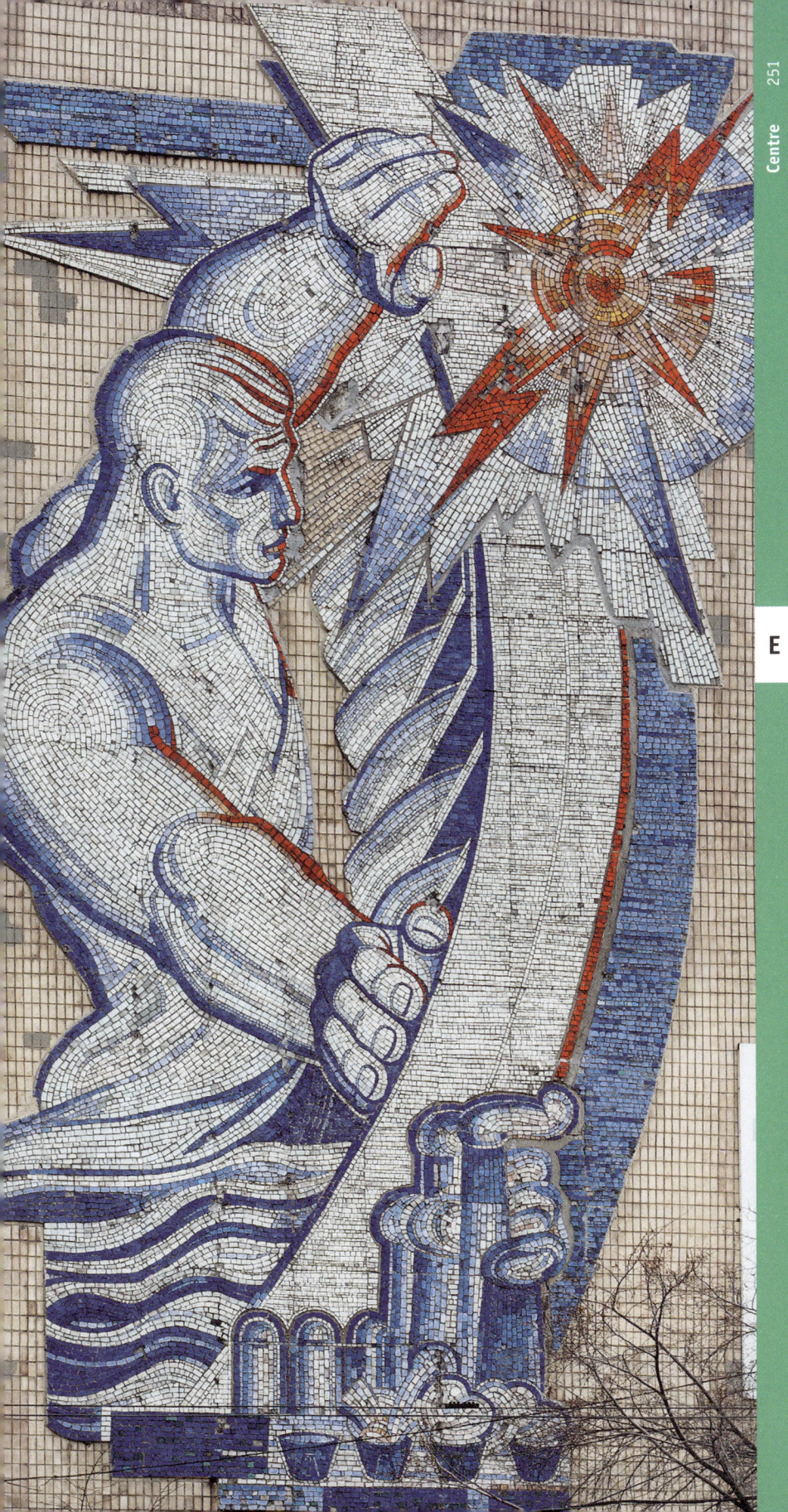

E

Autonomous State Fire Department no. 2

1A Zavodska Street,
Zaporizhzhia

Unknown artist
Smalt mosaic

106 E

The mosaic on the facade of the fire department celebrates traits commonly associated with the fireman profession – courage and dedication. In terms of style and subject, the artwork follows the standard representation of workers in the Soviet monumental and decorative arts. This mosaic is peculiar because the artists employed deeply saturated tint in the colour palette. The background behind the characters refers to the technical equipment necessary for the fulfilment of the firemen's duties. Its depiction varies from vividly figurative (in the corners) to abstract (in the centre).

Kryvorizhzhia Unit of Ukrtelecom

97 Heroiv ATO Street, Kryvyi Rih

107 **E**

Unknown artist
Ceramic mosaic, smalt mosaic,
concrete, relief, natural stone

Mosaics commissioned by factories, scientific institutes and communal service centres usually feature corresponding scenes of labour. This panel is maybe the only one dedicated to life of telephone operators, or 'switchers'. The artists depicted the actions, working area and even dresses of young female 'switchers' in detail, complementing the whole composition with decorative elements.

E

Welcome Stele to ArselorMitall Kryvyi Rih
7 Kryvorizhstal Street, Kryvyi Rih

Heorhii Bakhmutov
More Cast Iron, Steel and Rolled Stock for The Motherland (1979)
Ceramic mosaic, relief

This artwork by Heorhii Bakhmutov illustrates the aspiration for a 'synthesis of arts' in urban development. The artist merged both monumental and mosaic techniques within one space. Like many objects in the Dnipro region, where industrial enterprises are prevalent, this huge wall showcases the history of the plant, Kryvorizhstal. The factory was established in the 1930s on the edges of the Kryvyi Rih ironstone basin and initially was conceived of as a potential industrial giant, specialised in the production of cast iron, rolled metal and steel. The first blast furnace started operating on 4 August 1934, as the artwork informs the viewer. In 1939 Kryvorizhstal was awarded the Order of the Red Banner of Labour (an accurate image of the Order is seen near its corresponding inscription). On 24 April 1960, the plant's title was supplemented with the important specification 'named in honour of Lenin', granted as a part of his 90th anniversary of birthday celebrations. In 1971 Kryvorizhstal received the award which was considered the most prestigious in the Soviet Union – the Order of Lenin – one that is also pictured in the object. The inscription in the right bottom corner states in political-poster-like rhetoric: 'More Cast Iron, Steel and Rolled Stock for The Motherland.' Noteworthy, the artist portrayed the workers involved in distinct stages of production in a scanty colour palette, supplemented with turquoise outlines for the characters.

1934 год 4 августа
ДОМЕННАЯ ПЕЧЬ №1
КОМСОМОЛКА
ВЫДАЛА ПЕРВУЮ ПЛАВКУ
ЧУГУНА

1939 завод
НАГРАЖДЕН ОРДЕНОМ
ТРУДОВОГО
КРАСНОГО ЗНАМЕНИ
ЗАВОД НАГРАЖДЕН
ОМ ЛЕНИНА

РОДИНЕ БОЛЬШЕ
ЧУГУНА
СТАЛИ
ПРОКАТА

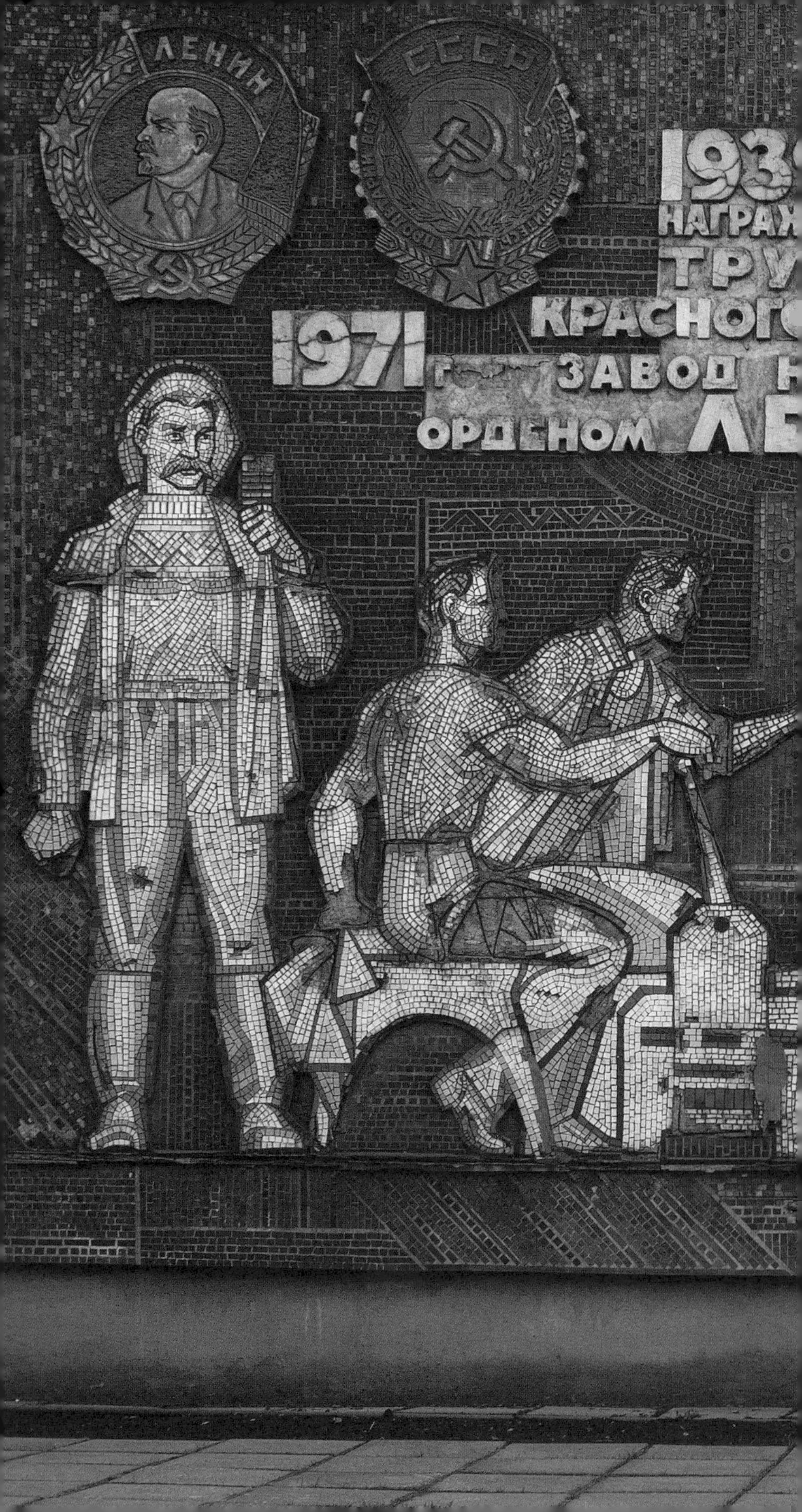
ЛЕНИН
СССР
1971
ЗАВОД
ОРДЕНОМ

**Residential Buildings
on Matusevicha Street**

31 Matusevycha Vitaliia Street,
Kryvyi Rih

Unknown artist
Ceramic mosaic, relief

109 E

This panel depicts three essential figures of the Soviet space program – Yuri Gagarin, Sergei Korolev and Valentina Tereshkova. It was probably created in the late 1960s or the early 1970s, when space enthusiasm was especially high and reflected in Soviet art. The notable feature of this mosaic is the pastel colour palette, rarely used in the depiction of cosmonauts.

E

Residential Buildings on Cherkasova Street

17-23 Cherkasova Street, Kryvyi Rih

 110 E

Anatolii Chernov, Heorhii Bakhmutov
Morning, Fertility, Family, Builders, On Guard (1965–1971)
Ceramic mosaic, smalt mosaic, concrete, relief, natural stone

The decoration of the five-storey residential buildings in Kryvyi Rih was created in five years by the artists Anatolii Chernov and Heorhii Bakhmutov, both educated in Moscow. Generally, the mosaic panels, placed on the silicate brick, depict conventional subjects in terms of Soviet visual culture – space and military achievements, the beauty of the daily life and the harmony in the family. The artworks are made on a relief of 10 to 20 centimetres, the surface of which was carved by hand in the places where concrete was applied (thus it resembles sgraffito). The artists used smalt, ceramic mosaics as well as tinted stone. One of the artworks illustrates the fertility of the local land where the woman, presumably, personifies Ukraine. Remarkably, the artists, especially in this mosaic panel, referred to the traditions of Ukrainian folk art and portrayed the characters in Ukrainian national costumes.[71]

E

Department Store

55/1 Bashtanskoi Respubliky,
Bashtanka

111 E

Unknown artist
Ceramic mosaic, broken ceramic ware

The astronaut was one of the most popular characters in Soviet mass culture after Gagarin's space flight in 1961. This composition demonstrates a humorous approach to the subject of space conquest: the astronaut is greeted by a girl in the national clothes with Sputnik in her bare hand. This panel is made with leftovers and broken pieces of simple household tiles.

Welcome Stele
Highway H11, Mykhailo-Laryne

Unknown artist
Ceramic mosaic

112 E

Boundary markers became widespread objects of small architecture and art in the 1970s. They were created by the Soviet government in order to indicate the limits of settlements or regions and to help drivers navigate through the less populated regions of the country. The mosaics on the boundary markers generally referred to the history of the region or, as in the case of the stele in Mykhailo-Laryne, depicted universally recognisable Soviet characters – workers and collective farmers (*kolhospnyky*). It is notable that the red banner at this boundary marker was repainted in Ukrainian and complemented with the national trident, apparently in the process of decommunisation.

E

House of Culture

1 Tsentralna Street, Taborivka

113 E

Unknown artist
Ceramic mosaic

The artists of this panel approached the subject of culture in a way unconventional to most Soviet Ukrainian monumental and decorative arts. They did not refer to local folk traditions but appropriated images associated with classical music to redefine canonical Soviet plot of 'the harmony of daily life'.

Voznesensk Shoe Factory
287 Kyivska Street, Voznesensk

114 E

Unknown artist
Smalt mosaic

The panels on the facade of the Voznesensk Shoe Factory demonstrate the complete process of footwear production. As one may discern, many Ukrainian monumental artists, including the creators of this mosaic, transformed the depiction of technological equipment and machinery into abstract backgrounds, filled with geometric patterns.

Yuzhnoukrainska Nuclear Power Plant
Car park of the Nuclear Power Plant, Yuzhnoukrainsk

Unknown artist
Smalt mosaic, relief, metal objects

115 E

The decoration of this nuclear power plant's facade is a remarkable example of an artwork which is not congruent with the doctrine of Socialist Realism. There is no portrayal of any human figure. It focuses on the depiction of rays – the wide yellow and orange lines emanating from the centre of the facade. The only element of Soviet visual culture one may notice in the mosaic is doves, which since the Sixth World Student and Youth Festival, held in 1957 in Moscow, were used in the Soviet Union as a symbol of peace (originating from Pablo Picasso's artwork). Their images in the panel hint at the benefits of nuclear power for the Soviet citizens. The nuclear power plant is a restricted access facility, so you need security's permission to take photos of the facade. But the entrance is open to the public.

E

Central Ukrainian National Technical University
8 Universytetskyi Avenue, Kropyvnytskyi

116 E

Anatolii Dvorskyi
Muse of Science
Smalt mosaic

The mosaic on the facade of the university employs a striking construction of the composition, one resembling Renaissance frescoes. We may suppose that the creation of the panel is linked with the general admiration of the heritage of 'great masters' (Michelangelo, Titian, Rubens) reflected in the 1970s in the Soviet and Ukrainian art publications.

Civil Registration Office

 **117** **E**

50 Sobornyi Avenue,
Oleksandriia

Artists: Ivan Lytovchenko,
Maria Lytovchenko, Volodymyr Priadka
Architects: M.Burkhanov, Y.Khorkhot
Sun of Love (1969)
Smalt mosaic, relief

According to the recollection of the artist Volodymyr Priadka, the initiator of the creation of the Civil Registration Office in Oleksandriia was Pavlo Chahanets, the chief construction engineer of the local charcoal industrial enterprise association, who was deeply in love with the town and aspired to support its multidimensional development. The object was built on the foundations of a two-storied building located next to the Shakhtar hotel. Priadka, the Lytovchenkos and Burkhanov were invited in 1968 to join the project team. The volumetric decoration of the facade, according to the intentions of the artists, is meant to convey the purity of love.[72] In the creation of the relief, Priadka and the Lytovchenkos for the first time in Ukrainian monumental practice used the methods of both oil painting and decorative plastics by applying the frame with a chain-link fence. The artwork is covered with the white smalt mosaic chips, painted in pastel yellow and blue.[73] The central figures of the relief are framed with geometric blocks that deliver to the viewer a sense of unity over the entire piece. The background is composed of Ukrainian folk symbols: oak leaves and bunches of viburnum. The former symbolises power, the latter evokes ideas of purity.[74] In the context of style and production technology, this piece proves an extraordinary token of Ukrainian monumental and decorative arts of the Soviet era.

E

![Sun of Love relief mosaic on building facade]

Mykhailo Ostrohradskyi Kremenchuk National University

20 Pershotravneva Street, Kremenchuk

Artist: Mykola Khakhin
Executors: M. Khakhin, A. Matrosov, N. Rudenko (1981)
Smalt mosaic

118 E

Images of scientists in Soviet monumental and decorative arts are somewhat theatrical, if not outright fantastical. Their suits, laboratories and props were deeply informed by science fiction aesthetics: more than mere practical implements, they singled scientists out as the masters of secret knowledge. Such an approach is underscored here by a bright palette, semi-abstract decorative elements and, as in the case of Kremenchuk National University, by unnatural yet grand-looking figures of scientists.

Commercial Bank (former Zhovtnevyi Cinema)

3 Soborna Street, Kremenchuk

119 E

Mykola Khakhin
Truth (1971–1974)
Smalt mosaic

This mosaic decorating the facade of the bank in Kremenchuk refers to the most famous Soviet newspaper, *Pravda* (*Truth*). After the release of the decree on 9 November 1917, which shut down all newspapers that opposed the Bolshevik regime, *Pravda* occupied the leading role in the provision of the Soviet people with 'proper' and 'accurate' news. Basically, the nationalisation of the press was an essential means to efficiently disseminate the Party's propaganda.[75] Remarkably, Mykola Khanin used titles of pre-revolutionary newspapers, distributed by Bolsheviks, to create the piece. Many of them, in particular, *Iskra* and *Proletariy*, considered as the predecessors of *Pravda*, were distributed illegally. One may notice a hint of irony in the execution of such an object in the era of distinct samizdat periodicals (derived from Russian 'self-publication'; implying the production and circulation of texts outside the framework of Soviet institutions).[76]

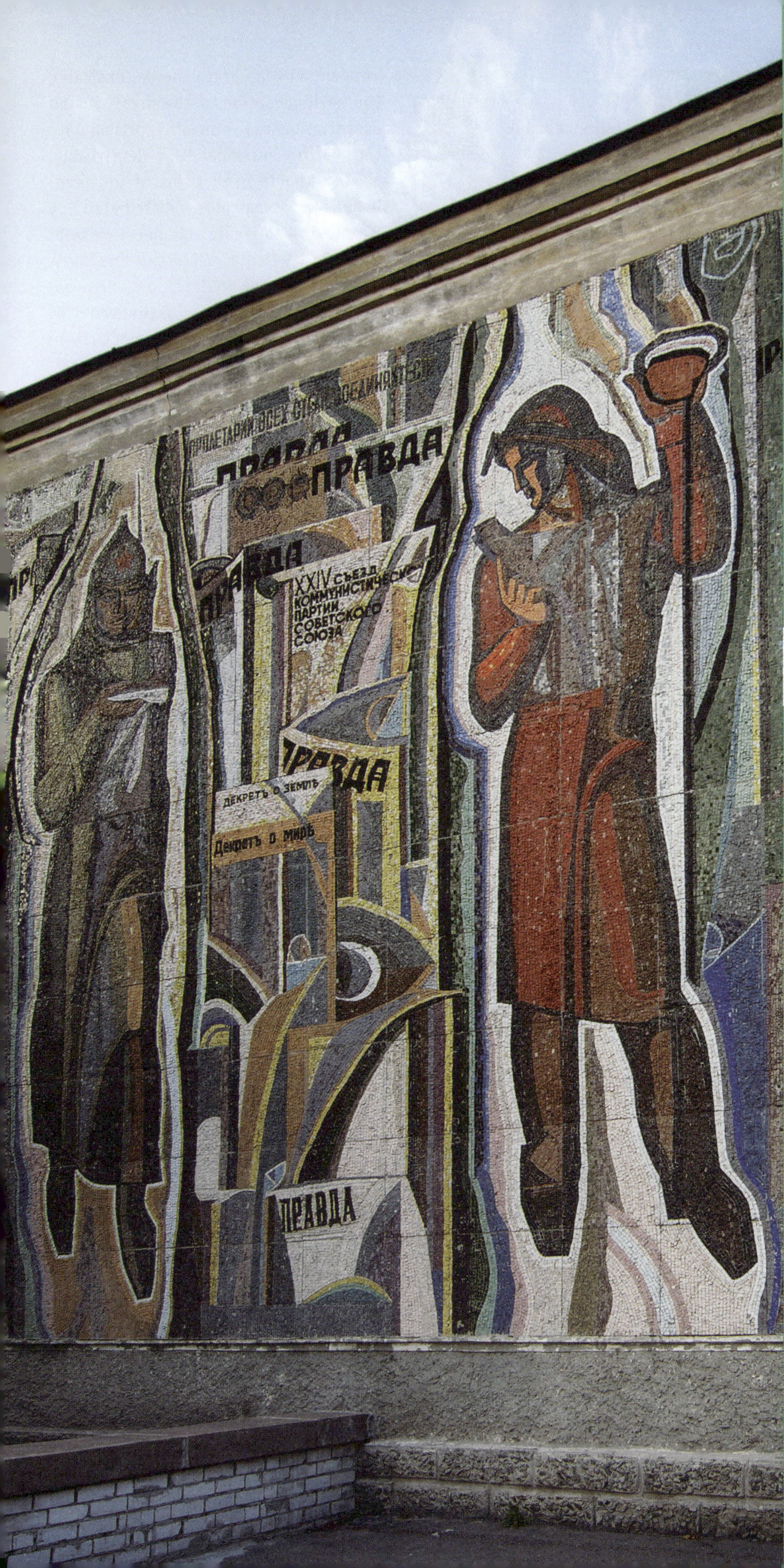
ПРОЛЕТАРИИ ВСЕХ СТРАН, СОЕДИНЯЙТЕСЬ!
ПРАВДА
ПРАВДА
ПРАВДА
XXIV СЪЕЗД КОММУНИСТИЧЕСКОЙ ПАРТИИ СОВЕТСКОГО СОЮЗА
ПРАВДА
ДЕКРЕТЪ О ЗЕМЛѢ
Декретъ о мирѣ
ПРАВДА

Polytechnic College at the Kremenchuk Mykhailo Ostrohradskyi National University

2 Myru Street, Horishni Plavni

Mykola Khakhin (1977)
Smalt mosaic

120 E

The Polytechnic College is decorated with another mosaic of Mykola Khaknin, visually uniting all campuses of the Kremenchuk Mykhailo Ostrohradskyi National University. This colossal panel depicts scientists in a phantasmagorical style. The artist left some figures incomplete and inscribed them into the abstract background. Notably, the vertical and horizontal lines which arrange the composition are repeated both on the characters' images and in the setting's space.

Khimik Palace of Culture

67 Viacheslava Chornovola
Street, Kamianske

`121` `E`

Valerii Lamakh, Ernest Kotkov
To the Sun (1971)
High relief, cement, ceramic mosaic

The Khimik (Chemist) Palace of Culture in Kamianske was one of the structures where Ernest Kotkov and Valerii Lamakh decorated both the interior and exterior. This artwork resembles the well-known panel at the Boryspil airport, *Icarus (The Human Conquers Sky)*, executed by the artists jointly with Ivan Lytovchenko in 1965. Indeed, *To the Sun*, as the Ukrainian art historian Halyna Skliarenko points out, incorporates features distinct to 'the style of the 1960s'.[77] However, in contrast to the mosaic at the Boryspil airport, the framework of this artwork does not impose the superiority of the straight lines in the composition. *To the Sun* is an airy panel, where Lamakh, who had already been working on *The Book of Schemes* for two years, tended to organise the space of the protruding relief in an ornamental way. The young couple, a boy and a girl, whose almost naked and sound bodies are highlighted with curved outlines, are reaching for the sun through the starry-night darkness, pictured in a schematic background. In 1975, the Soviet art historian Lidiya Popova stated that Lamakh was able to convey dynamism in the artwork through an unconventional solution: he shifted the volumetric object in relation to the central axis of the building.[78]

Endnotes

Introduction

1. Lodder, Christina, 'Lenin's Plan
   for Monumental Propaganda', in
   Bown, Matthew Cullerne and Taylor,
   Brandon (eds), *Art of the Soviets:
   Painting, Sculpture, and Architecture
   in a One-Party State, 1917-1992*
   (Manchester: Manchester University
   Press, 1993), pp. 16–32.
2. Bowlt, John, 'Russian Sculpture
   and Lenin's Plan of Monumental
   Propaganda, in Millon, H.A. and
   Nochlin, L. (eds), *Art and Architecture
   in the Service of Politics* (London: MIT
   Press, 1978), pp. 183-93.
3. Darewych, Daria. 'Soviet Ukrainian
   Painting c. 1955-1979: New Currents
   and Undercurrents', University
   College London, 1990.
4. Stalin, Joseph, 'XVI Sezd
   Kommunisticheskoi Partii Sovetskogo
   Soiuza [XVI Congress of The
   Communist Party of the Soviet
   Union].' *Pravda*, 27 June 1930.
5. For instance: Guldberg, Jørn,
   'Socialist Realism as Institutional
   Practice: Observations on the
   Interpretation of the Works of Art
   of the Stalin Period', in Gunther,
   Hans (ed), *The Culture of the Stalin
   Period* (Springer: 1990), pp. 149–177.
   And Heller, Leonid, 'A World of
   Prettiness: Socialist Realism and Its
   Aesthetic Categories', in Lahhusen,
   Thomas and Dobrenko, Evgenii
   Aleksandrovich (eds), *Socialist
   Realism Without Shores* (Duke
   University Press: 1997), pp. 51–75.
6. Brooks, Jeffrey, 'Socialist Realism
   in Pravda: Read All about It!'
   Slavic Review, vol. 53, no. 4, 1994,
   pp. 973-991.

7. Kornetchuk, Elena, 'Soviet Art under
   Government Control: From the 1917
   Revolution to Khrushchev's Thaw', in
   Rosenfeld, Alla and Dodge, Norton T.
   (eds), *Nonconformist Art: The Soviet
   Experience: 1956-1986* (New York:
   Thames and Hudson, 1995), pp. 36–49.
8. 'The Charter of the Union of Soviet
   Artists of Ukraine, 7 September
   1939', The Ukrainian Central State
   Archive-Museum of Literature and
   Art, Fund 581, Case 1.
9. Reid, Susan. 'Khrushchev in
   Wonderland: The Pioneer Palace
   in Moscow's Lenin Hills, 1962',
   in Müller, Andreas and Pietsch,
   Susanne (eds), *Walls that Teach*
   (Amsterdam: Japsam, 2014),
   pp. 127–156.

Regions

1. Korus, Elena, 'Monumentalnye proizvedeniya Valeria Lamakha i Ernesta
   Kotkova [Monumental Artworks
   of Valerii Lamakh and Ernest
   Kotkov]', *Antikvar*, <https://antikvar.
   ua/monumentalistika-lamaha-i-
   kotkova> accessed 1 June 2019.
2. Cooke, Catherine, 'Socialist Realist
   Architecture: Theory and Practice',
   in Brown, Matthew Cullerne and
   Taylor, Brandon, *Art of the Soviets:
   Painting, Sculpture, and Architecture
   in a One-Party State, 1917-1992*
   (Manchester: Manchester University
   Press, 1993), pp. 86–105.
3. Kettering, Karen, 'An Introduction
   to the Design of the Moscow Metro
   in the Stalin Period: The Happiness
   of Life Underground', *Studies in the
   Decorative Arts*, vol. 7, no. 2, Spring-
   Summer 2000, pp. 2–20.

4. Zaremba, F. M., Tselikovskaya, T. A., *Kievskiy metropoliten* [*Kyiv Underground Railway*] (Kyiv: Budivelnyk, 1976).
5. Cooke, Catherine, 'Socialist Realist Architecture: Theory and Practice', pp. 103.
6. Lahusen, Thomas, 'Socialist Realism in Search of Its Shores: Some Historical Remarks on the Historically Open Aesthetic System of the Truthful Representation of Life', in Lahusen, Thomas and Dobrenko, Evgenii Aleksandrovich (eds), *Socialist Realism Without Shores* (Duke University Press, 1997), pp. 5–26.
7. 'Korotka istoriia ta osnovni dosiah-nennia Instytutu yadernykh doslidz-hen NAN Ukrainy [The Brief History and Main Achievements of the Institute for Nuclear Research of the National Academy of Sciences of Ukraine]', The Institute for Nuclear Research, <http://www.kinr.kiev.ua/index.html> accessed 1 June 2019.
8. Bonnell, Victoria, *Iconography of Power: Soviet Political Posters Under Lenin and Stalin* (University of California Press, 1999).
9. 'Istoriia Muzeiu. Bohdan i Varvara Khanenky [The History of Museum. Bohdan and Varvara Khanenko]', Khanenko Museum, <http://khanenkomuseum.kiev.ua/istoriya-muzeyu/bogdan-i-varvara-hanenky> accessed 1 June 2019.
10. Ovchynnikov, Vasyl, 'Spohady pro navchannia u Kyivskomu khudozh-nomu instytuti [The Memoirs about Education at the Kyiv Art Institute]',

prepared and described by Kashuba-Volvach, Olena in *Suchasne mystet-stvo* [*Contemporary Art*], issue 7, 2010 (Kyiv: Modern Art Research Institute of Ukrainian Academy of Arts).
11. Rohdewald, Stefan, 'Post-Soviet Remembrance of the Holocaust and National Memories of the Second World War in Russia, Ukraine and Lithuania', *Forum for Modern Language Studies*, vol. 44, no. 2, 1 April 2008, pp. 173–84, <https://doi.org/10.1093/fmls/cqn007>.
12. 'Istoriia muzeiu [The History of Museum]', Memorial Complex National Museum of the History of Ukraine in the Second World War, <https://www.warmuseum.kiev.ua/ua/museum/history> accessed 1 June 2019.
13. O'Mahony, Mike, *Sport v SSSR. Fizicheskaya kultura – vizualnaya kultura* [*Sport in the USSR. Physical Culture – Visual Culture*] (Moscow: Novoe literaturnoe obozrenie, 2010).
14. Ibid., pp. 224.
15. Ibid.
16. Siegelbaum, Lewis H, 'The Shaping of Soviet Workers' Leisure: Workers' Clubs and Palaces of Culture in the 1930s', *International Labor and Working-Class History*, no. 56, 1999, pp. 78–92.
17. Dobrenko, Evgenii, *The Making of the State Reader: Social and Aesthetic Contexts of the Reception of Soviet Literature* (Stanford University Press, 1997).
18. Gerovitch, Slava, '"Why are We Telling Lies?": The Construction of Soviet Space History Myths,' in

Soviet Space Mythologies: Public Images, Private Memories, and the Making of a Cultural Identity, (Pittsburgh: University of Pittsburgh Press, 2015), pp. 1–26.

19. Ibid., pp. 157.

20. 'Istoriia universytetu [The History of the University]', Zhytomyr State Technological University, <https://ztu.edu.ua/ua/common/history.php> accessed 1 June 2019.

21. Chernyshova, Natalya, *Soviet Consumer Culture in the Brezhnev Era* (New York: Routledge, 2013).

22. Huliuk, Yevhen, 'Te, shcho vy mohly ne znaty pro lvivskyi "Okean" na Volodymyra Velykoho [Something You May Not Know About Lviv "Okean" on Volodymyra Velykoho Street]', *Galnet*, <https://galnet.fm/te-shho-vy-mogly-ne-znaty-pro-lvivskyj-okean-na-volodymyra-velykogo/> accessed 1 June 2019.

23. Ruble, Blair, *Soviet Trade Unions: Their Development in the 1970s* (Cambridge: Cambridge University Press, 2009).

24. 'Dunchak Attila', Brovdi Art <https://zakarpat.brovdi.art/khudozhnyky/myttsi-zakarpattia/dunchak-attila#parentHorizontalTab1> accessed 1 June 2019.

25. 'Keramika Ukrainy. Zakarpatskyi khudozhnii instytut. Viddilennia khudozhnoi keramiky [Ceramics of Ukraine. Transcarpathian Art Institute. Department of Art Ceramics]', *Professional Ceramics*, the website of Vydavnychyi tsentr Lohos Ukraina <http://www.logos.biz.ua/proj/keram/pdf/045.pdf> accessed 1 June 2019.

26. White, Anne, *De-Stalinization and the House of Culture: Declining State Control over Leisure in the USSR, Poland, and Hungary, 1953–89* (London: Routledge, 1990), pp. 21–22.

27. 'Pro teatr [About the theatre]', Ivan Franko Musical Drama Theatre in Ivano-Frankivsk <http://dramteatr.if.ua/category&category_id=12> accessed 1 June 2019.

28. 'Nashchadkam na zghadku: Keramichne panno Ivano-Frankivskoho dramteatru v detaliakh [A Keepsake for Descendants: the Ceramic Panel of Ivano Frankivsk Drama Theatre]', *Vezha*, <https://www.vezha.org/panno-drama/> accessed 1 June 2019.

29. Hrishyna, Tetiana, 'Protestnyi shtrykh: z farboiu na prezydenta [The Stroke of Protest: With Paint against the President]', *Volyn Post* <http://www.volynpost.com/articles/50-protestnyj-shtryh-z-farboyu-na-prezydenta> accessed 1 June 2019.

30. Yurko, Iryna, 'Pryzabute mystetstvo Ternopoli (Neimovirni foto) [Almost Forgotten Art of Ternopil (Brilliant Photos)]', *Realno*, 10 November 2017 <https://tinyurl.com/y4a8936y> accessed 1 June 2019.

31. Skliarenko, Halyna, *Ukrainski khudozhnyky: z vidlyhy do Nezalezhnosti [Ukrainian Artists: From the Thaw till the Independence]* (Kyiv: ArtHuss, 2018).

32. Lamakh, Valerii, *The Book of Schemes*, quoted in Skliarenko,

Halyna, *Ukrainski khudozhnyky: z vidlyhy do Nezalezhnosti* [*Ukrainian Artists: From the Thaw till the Independence*] (Kyiv: ArtHuss, 2018), pp. 71.

33. Ibid., pp. 74.
34. 'Istoriia muzeiu [The History of Museum]', Mykola Ostrovsky Regional Literary Memorial Museum <http://ostrovskymuseum.at.ua/index/0-11> accessed 1 June 2019.
35. Ibid.
36. 'Spysok osib, yaki pidpadaiut pid zakon pro dekomunizatsiiu [The List of the Individuals Who Fall within the Purview of the Decommunisation Law]', The Ukrainian Institute of National Remembrance <http://www.memory.gov.ua/publication/spisok-osib-yaki-pidpadayut-pid-zakon-pro-dekomunizatsiyu> accessed 1 June 2019.
37. Lishchenko, Lesia, 'Do istorii Khmelnytskoi AES ta Netishyna z naukovym pidkhodom [Scientific Approach to the History of the Khmelnytskyi Nuclear Power Plant and Netishyn]', *Perspektyva* [*Pespective*], 5 September 2017. <https://perspekt.org.ua/news/do-istorii-hmelnickoi-aes-ta-netishina-z-naukovim-pidhodom> accessed 1 June 2019.
38. 'Nasha biohrafiia [Our Biography]', Lutsk Driving School of the Ukrainian Defense Society <http://avtotsou-lutsk.yolasite.com/picture-gallery.php > accessed 1 June 2019.
39. Dzhiovani, V. N., and Urenov, V. P. 'Evolyutsiya razvitiya arhitekturno-planirovochnoy organizatsii Odesskogo zheleznodorozhnogo vokzala [The Evolution of Architectural-Planning Organisation of the Odessa Railway Station]', *Arkhitekturnyi visnyk KNUBA* [*The Kyiv National University of Building and Architecture Architectural Bulletin*], 2016 <https://tinyurl.com/y6z3afps> accessed 1 June 2019.
40. Radchenko, Olga, '"Inturist" v Ukraine 1960-1980 godov: mezhdu krasnoy propagandoy i tverdoy valyutoy [Intourist in Ukraine in the 1960-1980s: Between the Red Propaganda and Hard Currency]' (The Bohdan Khmelnytsky National University of Cherkasy, 2013).
41. Ibid., pp. 45.
42. 'Yastreb Lyudmila Lukinichna', Odesa Biographical Guide <http://odessa-memory.info/index.php?id=19> accessed 1 June 2019.
43. Hilton, Marjorie L., 'Retailing the Revolution: The State Department Store (GUM) and Soviet Society in the 1920s', *Journal of Social History*, vol. 4, 2004, pp. 939-964.
44. Knizhnik, R., and Levenberg, B. 'Novye tipy torgovyh i bytovyh zdaniy [New Types of Trade and Residential Buildings]', *Stroitelstvo i Arhitektura* [*Building and Architecture*], issue 2, 1958.
45. O'Mahony, *Sport v SSSR. Fizicheskaya kultura – vizualnaya kultura* [*Sport in the USSR. Physical Culture – Visual Culture*], pp. 224.
46. Ibid., pp. 235
47. Reid, 'Khrushchev in Wonderland: The Pioneer Palace in Moscow's Lenin Hills, 1962', pp. 146.

48. Ibid.
49. Ahaev, Aleksandr, *Imena Kryma. Etimologicheskiy slovar toponi- mov Kryma* [*The Names of Crimea. Etymological Dictionary of Crimea Toponyms*] (Hurzuf: 2011).
50. Zernova, Ekaterina, *Vospominaniya monumentalista* [*Memoirs of the Monumentalist*] (Moscow: Sovetskiy hudozhnik, 1985).
51. Reid, 'Khrushchev in Wonderland: The Pioneer Palace in Moscow's Lenin Hills, 1962', p. 143.
52. Wikipedia contributors, 'Pust vsegda budet solnce [May There Always Be Sunshine]', *Wikipedia, The Free Encyclopedia* <https://ru.wikipedia. org/?oldid=99998276> accessed 1 June 2019.
53. Reid, 'Khrushchev in Wonderland: The Pioneer Palace in Moscow's Lenin Hills, 1962', p. 146.
54. Karakis, I., and Gorodskoy, V, 'Ot eksperimenta – k massovomu stroi- telstvu [From the Experiment to the Mass Construction]', *Stroitelstvo i Arhitektura* [*Building and Architecture*], issue 11, 1960.
55. Cherny, Robert W, *Victor Arnautoff and the Politics of Art* (University of Illinois Press, 2017).
56. Arnautoff, Victor, *Zhizn Zanovo* [*Life Anew*] (Donetsk: Donbas Publishing House, 1972).
57. Plaksii, Borys, 'Liudyna bez stra- khu [The Person without Fear]', in *Chervona tin kalyny: Lysty, spohady, statti* [*The Red Shadow of Viburnum: Letters, Memoirs, Articles*], Zaretskyi, Oles and Marychevskyi, Mykola (eds) (Kyiv: Spalakh LTD, 1996).
58. Bykov, Alex, and Gubkina, Ievgeniia, *Soviet Modernism, Brutalism, Post- Modernism: Building and Structures in Ukraine 1955–1991* (Kyiv: Osnovy Publishing, DOM Publishers).
59. Ibid., p. 35.
60. Bahmet, Tatyana, 'Vitaliy Ivanovich Lenchin – hudozhnik i peda- gog [Vitalii Ivanovych Lenchyn – the Artist and the Pedagog]', Konstantin Stanislavski Kharkiv Specialised Music and Theatre Library <http://www.mtlib.org. ua/ukazateli/40-vitalij-ivanovich- lenchin.html> accessed 1 June 2019.
61. O'Mahony, *Sport v SSSR. Fizicheskaya kultura – vizualnaya kultura* [*Sport in the USSR. Physical Culture – Visual Culture*], pp. 32-37.
62. Kokshaykin, M.G., and Korotchenko, B.Y, 'Istoriya Shostkinskogo kazen- nogo zavoda Zvezda [The History of the Star Shostka State Plant]', Shostka.org <http://shostka. ho.ua/history/history-zvezda> accessed 1 June 2019.
63. Brooks, 'Socialist Realism in Pravda: Read All about It!', p. 983.
64. Kokshaykin, M.G. '"SVEMA" – stranicy istorii ["Svema" – the Pages of History]', Shostka.org<http://shostka. ho.ua/history/history-svema> accessed 1 June 2019.
65. 'The Thematic Plan and the List of Artworks of the Republican Anniversary Exhibition, Dedicated to the 40th Anniversary of the Great Socialist October Revolution: 1957', The Ukrainian Central State Archive- Museum of Literature and Art, Fund 581, Case 625.
66. Chervonenko, Vitalii, '"Za Lenina,

za Stalina": yak na Chernihivshchyni berezhut portrety "vozhdiv"["For Lenin, For Stalin": How the Portraits of "Chieftains" Are Preserved in the Chernihiv Region]', *BBC News Ukraine*, 13 August 2018 <https://www.bbc.com/ukrainian/features-45173635> accessed 1 June 2019.

67. Wikipedia contributors, 'Neperspektyvni sela [Unpromising Villages]', *Wikipedia, The Free Encyclopedia* <https://tinyurl.com/yydvojtk> accessed 1 June 2019.

68. German, Lizaveta, 'Alla Horska, "Prapor Peremohy" [Alla Horska, "The Victory Banner"]', in Yakovlenko, Kateryna (ed), *Why There Have Been Great Women Artists in Ukrainian Art* (ed) (Kyiv: Publish Pro, 2019), pp. 128–137.

69. Korus, 'Monumentalnye proizvedeniya Valeriia Lamakha i Ernesta Kotkova [Monumental Artworks of Valerii Lamakh and Ernest Kotkov]'.

70. Wikipedia contributors, 'Dneproges [Dnipro Hydroelectric Station]', *Wikipedia, The Free Encyclopedia* <https://ru.wikipedia.org/?oldid=99758391> accessed 1 June 2019.

71. Vashchenko, Maryna, 'Tvorchyi shliakh khudozhnyka-monumentalista Anatoliia Chernova [The Creative Path of the Artist-Monumentalist Anatolii Chernov]', *Visnyk Lvivskoi akademii mystetstv [The Lviv National Academy of Arts Bulletin]*, issue 24.

72. Karpacheva, Elena, '"Gimn zhizni" pod "Solncem lyubvi" ["Hymn to Life" under the "Sun of Love"]', *Oleksandriiskyi Tyzhden (The Week of Oleksandria)*, 16 August 2016 <http://ot.kr.ua/gimn-zhizni-pod-solntsem-lyubvi.html> accessed 1 June 2019l.

73. Korus, 'Monumentalnye proizvedeniya Valeriia Lamakha i Ernesta Kotkova [Monumental Artworks of Valerii Lamakh and Ernest Kotkov]'.

74. Karpacheva, '"Gimn zhizni" pod "Solncem lyubvi" ["Hymn to Life" under the "Sun of Love"].'

75. Brooks, Jeffrey, *Thank You, Comrade Stalin! Soviet Public Culture from Revolution to Cold War* (Princeton University Press, 2001).

76. Ledeneva, Alena, T*he Global Encyclopaedia of Informality*, Volume 1, 2018 <http://www.oapen.org/record/642570> accessed 1 June 2019.

77. Skliarenko, *Ukrainski khudozhnyky: z vidlyhy do Nezalezhnosti [Ukrainian Artists: From the Thaw till the Independence]*, 65.

78. Popova, Lidiya, 'Hudozhniki-monumentalisty Ukrainy [The Artists-Monumentalists of Ukraine],' *Sovetskoe monumentalnoe iskusstvo-73* (Moscow: Sovetskiy hudozhnik, 1975).

Index of Places

Digits indicate project numbers

Index of Persons

Digits indicate project numbers

House of Culture (1981). Rashivka, Poltava Region

Authors

Yevgen Nikiforov

is a Ukrainian visual artist, a director and
a documentary photographer. He started
his professional photography practice in
2005. Since 2013 Yevgen has been working on independent documentary projects. His current projects are 'Ukrainian
Soviet Mosaics' (2013–2020) and 'On
Republic's Monuments' (2014–2019).
Yevgen is the author of the book
Decommunized: Ukrainian Soviet Mosaics.
One of the major subjects he has been
working on for four years is Soviet cultural heritage, which remains in towns
all across Ukraine, and the controversial
attitudes towards it today.

Polina Baitsym

is a Ukrainian art historian and a curator
who promotes a research-based approach
to exhibitions. Since 2017 she has been
exploring the institutional framework
of Socialist Realism in Ukraine in Soviet
times. Her primary research interests
are national art histories and the development of art historical disciplines. In
2018 Polina launched a research initiative dedicated to Ukrainian children's
illustration from the 1960 to the 1990s.
Currently, she is a PhD student at Central
European University.

Acknowledgements

Lizaveta German, Olha Balashova,
Oleksiy Bykov, Vladyslav Zaitsev,
Olena Korus, Elena Likhovodova,
Oleksandr Nikitchuk, Oleksandr Chernov,
Inna Kozyreva, Danyil Holovko,
Volodymyr Melnychenko, Elena Zaretska,
Varvara Podnos, Valentyn Onyshchenko,
Illya Kannunikov, Yuriy Nischenko

With the support of
Goethe-Institut Ukraine

The *Deutsche Nationalbibliothek* lists this publication in the *Deutsche National bibliografie*;
detailed bibliographic data are available at
http://dnb.d-nb.de.

ISBN 978-3-86922-601-9 (2nd edition)

© 2022 by DOM publishers, Berlin
www.dom-publishers.com

Research, photographer
Yevgen Nikiforov

Texts
Polina Baitsym

Final Proofreading
Elisha Meir Aaron

Layout
Serhiy Mishakin

Maps
Katrin Soschinski

QR-Codes
Christoph Gößmann

Photo credits
Unless otherwise stated, all the pictures were taken by
Yevgen Nikiforov
Siniavin, Valentyn: 097D;
Stepanenko, Anastasia: 098D

Printing
Bilnet Matbaacılık ve Yayıncılık A. Ş., Istanbul
www.bilnet.net.tr